CW00554881

Secret Casualties of World War Two

Secret Casualties of World War Two

Uncovering the Civilian Deaths from Friendly Fire

Simon Webb

First published in Great Britain in 2020 by
Pen & Sword History
An imprint of
Pen & Sword Books Ltd
Yorkshire - Philadelphia

ISBN 978 1 52674 322 0

A CIP catalogue record for this book is available from the British Library.

Typeset in 11.5/14 Ehrhardt by Vman Infotech Pvt. Ltd.

Printed and bound in England by TJ International Ltd.

Pen & Sword Books Ltd incorporates the Imprints of Pen & Sword Archaeology, Atlas, Aviation, Battleground, Discovery, Family History, History, Maritime, Military, Naval, Politics, Railways, Select, Transport, True Crime, Fiction, Frontline Books, Leo Cooper, Praetorian Press, Seaforth Publishing, Wharncliffe and White Owl.

For a complete list of Pen & Sword titles please contact

PEN & SWORD BOOKS LIMITED
47 Church Street, Barnsley, South Yorkshire, S70 2AS, England
E-mail: enquiries@pen-and-sword.co.uk
Website: www.pen-and-sword.co.uk

or

PEN AND SWORD BOOKS
1950 Lawrence Rd, Havertown, PA 19083, USA
E-mail: uspen-and-sword@casematepublishers.com
Website: www.penandswordbooks.com

Contents

List of Illustrations

18. Grave of a nurse from Shropshire who was a friendly-fire casualty in the Blitz.
19. Plaque at Bethnal Green Tube station, commemorating the 'worst civilian disaster of the Second World War'.
20. Plaque at the railway bridge across Grove Road, marking the spot where the first V 1 landed in London.

Introduction

The relentless and ferocious aerial bombing raids launched against Britain by the German air force or Luftwaffe between September 1940 and May 1941 are remembered today as the Blitz. The Blitz occupies a place of honour in British history, a special myth which is still very precious for the light which it supposedly sheds on Britain and the nature of its people at that time. Other aspects of Britain's imperial past may be mocked or derided, but seldom the Blitz. It remains, 80 years later, more or less sacrosanct, immune from the iconoclasm which has shattered so many other popular legends which were at one time beloved of the British nation. The Blitz is different.

There is, however, a serious problem with the carefully, one might almost say cunningly, constructed narrative which lies at the heart of the Blitz as we know it. It is not merely that it is almost wholly false – many heroic legends are that. The chief difficulty with the story of the Blitz, as it has been handed down to us and carefully embellished over the years, is that it conceals a terrible crime, the massacre, by their own armed forces, of thousands of British civilians.

Before going any further, it might be profitable to read two accounts of air raids during the Second World War. One of these took place in England in 1940, at the height of the Blitz, and the other describes the Japanese attack on the American naval base of Pearl Harbor and subsequent deaths in Hawaii at the end of 1941. The first source is a quotation from a recently published book about the Women's Royal Naval Service (Neil R. Storey, *WRNS: The Women's Royal Naval Service*, Shire Publications 2017):

> Among the major incidents were the deaths of ten Wrens serving with HMS *Daedalus*, RNAS Station, Lee-on-Solent, when their hotel received a direct hit during an air raid on 14 September 1940.

The second is part of an eyewitness account of the devastation in Honolulu, capital of Hawaii, during the Japanese attack on Pearl Harbor in 1941. It was written a week after the events described, by Elizabeth P. McIntosh, a reporter for the *Honolulu Star-Bulletin*.

> Bombs were still dropping over the city as ambulances screamed off into the heart of the destruction. The drivers were blood-sodden when they returned, with stories of streets ripped up, houses burned, twisted shrapnel and charred bodies of children.

At first sight, there is no connection between these two incidents, other than that they both involve deaths during air raids by, respectively, German and Japanese forces, but in fact they are linked in a horrifying and unexpected fashion. The ten members of the Women's Royal Naval Service who died in the English town of Lee-on-Solent in 1940 did indeed die when 'their hotel reccived a direct hit during an air raid', but they were not killed by a German bomb, even though an air raid was taking place at the time. They and a dozen other women were sitting round the dining table at their billet in the Mansfield House Hotel, when an anti-aircraft shell crashed into the building and exploded in the room where they were sitting. The shell had been fired by British artillery in nearby Portsmouth. Similarly, the death and destruction in Honolulu in 1941 was caused not by Japanese bombs, but by 5in naval guns fired at the attacking Japanese aeroplanes by American sailors. Both incidents were classic examples of what is sometimes known as 'friendly fire' or 'collateral damage'.

Our exploration of aerial warfare and the civilian casualties which sometimes result from it will perhaps benefit from a preliminary word or two about the terminology used. The subject of this book is civilians who were killed by their own side during the Second World War. There are various euphemisms for the phenomenon of soldiers accidentally killing their comrades; fratricide, amicide, friendly fire and blue on blue being a few of them. These all carry the connotation of military casualties, in other words soldiers being killed by soldiers. Unwanted civilian casualties are sometimes referred to, by the Americans in particular, as 'collateral damage'. This expression is used for all unintended civilian deaths and damage to civil property, whether belonging to the enemy or to allies. The United States Department of Defense has defined collateral damage as, 'unintentional or incidental injury or damage to persons or objects that would not be lawful military targets in the circumstances ruling at the time'. This seems a monstrously callous and cold-blooded way of referring to the death of both adults and children, lumping them all in with broken windows and damaged roofs, and, for that reason, will not be used here.

The commonly-accepted definition of the term 'friendly fire' specifically excludes non-combatants, but I have chosen to use it in this book because most readers will be familiar with the expression and understand that it means damage, injuries and deaths inadvertently inflicted on one's own side. I have simply extended the term to embrace civilians.

Civilian deaths from friendly fire during the Second World War were alarmingly widespread and common. Almost 75 years later though, it is sometimes thought to be a little tactless and in poor taste to mention them. British civilians blown to pieces by German bombs are one thing, those killed by artillery fired by their own side are another matter entirely. Similarly, when we recall the Normandy landings on D-Day, we are probably vaguely aware that some French civilians inevitably became casualties. Nobody really wishes to hear though that the British and American forces killed as many French civilians that day as they did German soldiers.

The deaths of those civilians killed by their own side is often obscured by enemy action taking place at the same time. So it is that that peering through what is sometimes called the 'fog of war' can be a confusing and misleading experience, and we find ourselves in a muddle about what has actually happened and who was killed by whom. It might make the subject-matter of this book a little clearer if we conduct what the Germans call a *gedankenexperiment*, a thought experiment. First, a little background information.

In a situation where bombs are being dropped from aeroplanes and artillery shells are being fired up at those aircraft, there may be so many explosions taking place that it will seem hopeless to find out just what is going on. Beginning with the British experience of the Blitz, let us forget for a moment all about bombs being dropped from aeroplanes and consider only what the British Army was doing, in and around the nation's cities, especially between 1940 and 1944. I want readers to imagine, to begin with, that we have decided to set up hundreds of heavy artillery pieces both in the middle of London and also around the edge of the city. When I say 'heavy', I mean *really* heavy.

Illustration 1 shows a pair of heavy guns on HMS *King George V*, the flagship of the British fleet during the Second World War. These Quick Firing (QF) 5.25in guns were fearsome weapons and perfectly suited to naval warfare. They could hurl a shell weighing 80lbs (36.3kg) over 13 miles and were capable of penetrating armour which was 3in thick. Nothing more useful could be desired, if you wished to lob high explosives at enemy ships. If you struck your target, then all well and good. Should your shell fall short or overshoot, only a mighty splash would be caused in the surrounding ocean. It is hard to believe that anybody in his senses who would think it a wise and prudent decision to take one of these armoured gun turrets off a battleship and plonk it down in the middle of a city, using it then to fire shells not at slow-moving warships, but rather at fast-moving and agile aircraft flying above the streets. Nevertheless, this is precisely what was done in London.

Illustration 2 is of just such a gun turret on the top of Primrose Hill, overlooking London Zoo. It shows a pair of QF 5.25in guns, not on a battleship at sea, but in the heart of the capital. Ideally, the shells projected from this gun will explode thousands of feet in the air above London. Around half the time-delay fuzes used in these artillery shells are defective though, which means that although they are intended to set the shells off when they are high over the city, they often fail to do so and the shells will instead explode in the streets of the capital. Illustrations 12 and 13 show two more gun turrets which have been removed from warships and set down in London. These are QF 4.5in naval guns.

The shells which do explode at 20,000ft or more produce masses of chunks of steel, some of them little splinters and others heavy lumps like the one in Illustration 3, which shows the nosecone of a 3.7in anti-aircraft shell weighing a little over a pound (0.5kg). This particular example landed in a London garden at a speed of around 200 miles per hour in 1940. The smaller pieces of artillery shells, weighing just an ounce or two, are also quite capable of causing injury or death if they hit the right part of the body. This means that even if a shell behaves just as it is supposed to and explodes at the correct height, it still poses a mortal hazard to those in the streets below. As for the 80lb shells which fall to the ground and explode, they are absolutely lethal and could easily destroy a house, killing all those within.

Other naval guns used in London, such as the 4.5in, fired shells which weighed 55lbs (25kg). The most common anti-aircraft artillery used at that time in Britain had a calibre of 3.7in, the shells of which weighed 28lbs (12.7 kg). A 3.7in anti-aircraft gun may be seen in Illustration 4. Having positioned our heavy artillery around London, we will, just to make things more interesting, add a few hundred other guns, these firing explosive projectiles weighing only 2lbs (1kg) or so. Illustration 15 shows a pair of such weapons, the Bofors gun. As with the larger shells, some will explode in the air and others on the ground. We are now ready to start one of the most sustained artillery barrages the world has ever seen. We will fire 10,000, 12,000 or 13,000 shells into the air each night, for months on end, and hope that we do not cause too many casualties.

We know that many of the shells used had defective time fuzes, but two more factors made the situation even more even more dangerous for Londoners. One of these is the fact that the men operating the artillery were often not of the highest quality. Some were from the Home Guard, but even the soldiers from the regular army were those which no other unit was keen to have, men whom General Pile, head of the anti-aircraft force, described candidly as, 'the leavings of the Army intake'. Consider, for instance, the 31st AA Brigade. Out of a thousand recruits, fifty could not be used for duty because they were unsafe to be allowed out on their own. Twenty were mentally defective, what we would today call learning disabled, and eighteen had such severe medical conditions that they were really medically unfit for any other unit other than the anti-aircraft brigade. It was men of this sort who would be relied upon to use complicated equipment to establish the height and bearing of enemy bombers, carry out difficult calculations and then set the fuzes on artillery shells correctly, so as to ensure that they exploded in mid-air and not on the ground.

The other thing which greatly increased the chances of civilians being killed was the sheer number of shells being fired into the sky above London. On 14 October 1940, a total of 8,326 shells were fired in the London area and this was by no means the heaviest barrage. At other times, over

13,500 shells were fired in the course of an eight-hour barrage. Night after night, around 10,000 shells went up and either exploded and showered the city with lethal shrapnel or came down again and exploded like bombs in the streets of London.

This then is our 'thought experiment'. I want readers to imagine that for months at a time we use the artillery described above to shell London and other cities. This will be one of the heaviest artillery bombardments the world has ever known. In the week before the troops went 'over the top' on the Somme in 1916, the British artillery rained down a total of 1,738,000 shells onto the German positions. This is far less than the number of shells fired over London in 1940 and 1941. Forgetting for a moment about any bombs also being dropped from aeroplanes, readers are invited to consider what they think the consequences of this dreadful artillery barrage alone might have been for those on the streets of the capital.

So far, without any German involvement, I have been describing a terrible Blitz on the cities of Britain, one which was concealed by the chaos surrounding the drone of enemy aircraft and the dropping of their own bombs. Everybody knows that German bombs were exploding and killing people, but hardly anybody ever stops to think about the hundreds of tons of high-explosive shells which were also being fired at the same time. The big question is of course, how many of the civilians who died in Britain during German air raids were actually killed by artillery fired by their own side? It is this question which will attempt to answer in this book. There has never been any dispute about the fact that more British civilians were killed by the artillery than German aircrew. The estimates range from perhaps 10 per cent to as many as 50 per cent of the deaths on the ground during air raids being the result of British forces, rather than the Germans. This latter figure was one favoured by the men working frantically on the development of the proximity fuze, which would ensure that a shell exploded only when it was near enough to an aeroplane to cause serious damage to it. A scientist working on this idea at the Cavendish Laboratories calculated that half the time-fuzes used in anti-aircraft shells were defective and that as a result, they might be killing at least as many people during an air raid as were dying from the German bombs. If this figure were to be true, then it would mean that British anti-aircraft artillery was directly responsible for the death of over 26,000 civilians in Britain during the course of the Second World War.

Fully to understand the catastrophe which anti-aircraft fire wrought, both in Britain and America, we must first look back to the nineteenth century and see how the idea of deterring aircraft by the use of guns originated. Chapter 1 traces this notion from the earliest times up until the start of the First World War in 1914. By that time strategic bombing, that is to say attacks by aeroplanes on the means of production and the enemy's general ability to wage war, had become a recognized strand in the use of air power. Thought was also being given to ways in which enemy aircraft could be deterred from flying over one's own territory.

Chapter 1

A Brief History of Aerial Warfare Before 1914

For almost the whole of human history, warfare has been a two-dimensional activity. Armies, and individual soldiers, can move back and forth or from side to side, but they cannot move up and down. This restriction on mobility, which at first sight seems so obvious as to be hardly worth stating explicitly, has had profound implications during time of war, particularly in the last century or so, for defence against bombs dropped from aeroplanes.

Aerial bombardment of one kind or another, that is to say objects being projected onto armies, castles or towns from above, has been around for thousands of years. The only countermeasures available were, until the modern age, purely defensive. The Roman army, for instance, had a well-practised response to a rain of arrows from above or rocks hurled down upon troops when they were assaulting a walled position or travelling through a ravine. The soldiers were ordered to lock their shields together, over their heads and at the sides of the body of troops. This was the *testudo* or tortoise formation and it meant that arrows and other missiles coming from above, simply bounced off the shields. This of course protected the men, but did not deter the enemy from their attacks. Nor was it possible to strike back against the assault from above.

The ancient Greeks devised siege engines which could hurl rocks for a considerable distance into defended forts or town. There was no practical defence against such weapons and those under such a barrage could only hope that none of the rocks or small boulders would hit them. The Romans also used such catapults, and similar devices, such as trebuchets, were popular in medieval Europe. One point to bear in mind, and we shall return to this in the next chapter, is that it did not particularly matter to the operators of such siege engines if their machines were at all accurate. After all, as long as the rocks were launched in the general direction of the enemy, that was all that mattered. If a boulder hit a wall, it would cause damage, and anybody who was struck during such an assault was sure to be one of the enemy. This was the position too with gunpowder weapons, early artillery, when they appeared in the Middle Ages. A cannon ball fired towards the enemy army was sure to do harm to the enemy, rather than to one's own side.

We have outlined above two ideas which will be crucial to the understanding of the subject of this book, which is to say the horrifying number of their own civilians, and those of allied nations, killed by the British and American armies during the Second World War. The first is that before the advent of balloons and aeroplanes, weapons of war designed to kill or cause damage at a distance needed just two measurements to guide them to a target, namely how far the projectile would need to be sent and in what direction. This is because a battlefield, either on land or at sea, or the siege of a castle or town, all take place essentially in two dimensions and so two coordinates are sufficient to pinpoint any target. The second thing to consider is that when you are firing artillery of any kind towards enemies, accuracy is not crucial. When the artillery barrage was directed at German lines in the days before the Battle of the Somme in 1916, it did not really matter at all if any shell hit a particular spot. The important thing was that they pounded the area where the German soldiers were sheltering. In the same way, a shell which either did not explode at all or exploded some time after impact was also not a disaster. This was because all the shells were falling on enemy territory.

The first suggestion of bombing from aircraft as a possible method of warfare dates, surprisingly, from the seventeenth century, over a hundred years before the first manned flight in a hot air balloon. In 1663 an Italian priest called Francesco Lana de Terzi came up with an ingenious idea for a flying machine. He thought that if all the air was to be evacuated from four enormous and very thin copper spheres, then they would be much lighter than the surrounding atmosphere. If they were harnessed to a boat, then the natural buoyancy of the four vacuum-filled globes in the surrounding air could lift the boat and take passengers up into the sky. Of course, what would really happen would be that the pressure of the air around them would crush the spheres, if they contained vacuums within them. This did not stop the Jesuit priest from speculating freely upon the uses to which such an aerial vessel might be put.

One of the most prescient of Francesco Lana de Terzi's ideas was that an airship of the kind which he described would be useful for an attacking army. He wrote that, 'no city would be safe from raids' and went on to suggest that, 'fireballs and bombs could be hurled from a great height'. Because of such horrors, the pious priest decided that God would never allow any such craft to be constructed by men. In this he was of course mistaken.

The first manned flights of balloons, those constructed by the Montgolfier brothers, which used hot air, took place in November 1783. It was a shade under 11 years before anybody thought of putting such balloons to use for military purposes. During the Battle of Fleurus in Belgium, in the summer of 1794, Captain Coutelle of the French army went up in a balloon to observe what the enemy army was up to. It was for observations of this sort that first balloons and then aeroplanes, were to become very useful for armies.

The world's first airborne bombing raid was conducted by the Austrian Army against the Italian city of Venice, which they were besieging in 1849. On 22 August that year, the Austrians launched unpiloted hot air balloons, each carrying a bomb weighing 30lbs (14kg). The hope was that the wind would carry these balloon bombs, which were fitted with slow-burning fuzes, into the besieged city. In the event, the wind changed and blew the balloons back towards those who had launched them. The Austrians found themselves, therefore, in great danger from this early instance of friendly fire. The balloon bombs all exploded without causing anybody any harm, as an eyewitness described:

> The balloons appeared to rise to about 4,500ft. Then they exploded in mid-air or fell into the water, or, blown by a sudden southeast wind, sped over the city and dropped on the besiegers. Venetians, abandoning their homes, crowded into the streets and squares to enjoy the strange spectacle.

Although the balloons exploded chiefly over the Austrians, nobody was hurt. A second attempt was equally unsuccessful and it was to be almost a century before this particular experiment was repeated.

In November 1944, by which time it was obvious to most people that Japan had lost the war, a last-ditch attempt was made to attack the Americans in their own country. A fleet of hydrogen balloons, 9,000 of them, were launched into the jet stream which travels across the Pacific Ocean. Each balloon carried an anti-personnel bomb weighing 33lbs (15kg). All but 1,000 fell into the sea during the course of the 6,000-mile journey and the only casualties were a woman and five children picnicking in woods in the state of Oregon, all of whom were killed when one of the bombs exploded near them.

It is not generally known that the British army launched incendiary balloon bombs of this sort against Germany in 1941 and 1942, with some success in starting fires. A huge floating minefield was also set up during the Second World War, consisting of 900 balloons each carrying a bomb. These were supposed to catch German aircraft by drawing up bombs to explode, if one of the wired was snagged. An account of this device will be found in a later chapter.

The Union Army during the American Civil War made use of balloons for observation and in fact operated the world's first aircraft carrier to get the balloons from place to place. If we take as a definition of an aircraft carrier that it is a waterborne craft used to tether, transport or launch an aircraft, the converted coal barge *G W Parke Custis* certainly falls into the category. She towed observation balloons along the Potomac river in 1861, spying on the movement of the Confederate forces on the opposite bank of the river. Nine years later came a development in the field of warfare which is greatly germane to our investigation. This was the use of the world's first anti-aircraft gun.

The Franco-Prussian War of 1870–1 is today an all but forgotten footnote in European history. A Prussian army invaded France and encircled Paris. What is of interest is what happened once the French capital city was completely besieged, on 19 September 1870, with nobody able to enter or leave. Just four days after the Prussian Army had secured a blockade around Paris, the balloon *Neptune* took off and sailed over the Prussian lines, carrying over 250lbs of mail. After Paris was besieged, the French established a provisional government at the city of Tours and it was important to maintain communication between that city and the capital.

The Prussians were, not unnaturally, furious to see their siege being broken so easily and a fusillade of rifle fire was directed at the balloon, to no avail. The success of this first flight encouraged the French to establish a regular postal service out of Paris. There were sixty-six balloon flights out of the city during the siege and the Prussians grew increasingly frustrated and angry about them. In addition to carrying letters, information was being transmitted to the French military forces and over 100 people were also able to leave Paris in this way.

Having found that ordinary rifles were useless when it came to bringing down balloons, the Prussians sent word to the German armaments manufacturer Alfred Krupp. His company set about making the first anti-aircraft gun the world had ever seen. The *Ballonabwehrkanone* or balloon defence cannon, was a 37mm breech-loading gun, which was mounted on a wheeled vehicle, so that it could be moved to wherever it was most needed. This weapon may be seen in Illustration 5. An important point to note is that this gun fired large-calibre bullets, not explosive shells. The most significant thing about the *Ballonabwehrkanone* is that it suggested to future generations that it was possible for forces on the ground to tackle aircraft by shooting up at them. In other words, for the first time in history, the idea was mooted that a defence was possible to attacks from above. Not of course that the French balloons posed any sort of threat to the Prussian army, but the principle of being able to attack an airborne object was in this way established. It was claimed by the Prussians that five balloons were shot down with this weapon, but that is unlikely. Often, the balloons would land of their own accord and the Prussians would immediately claim that they had been brought down by their efforts. Only one balloon was definitely hit and disabled by this, the first ever anti-aircraft gun. The anti-aircraft gun thus predated the bomber by over 40 years.

It was not until the flight of the first Zeppelin airship in 1900, and the invention of a practical, heavier-than-air flying machine by the Wright brothers in 1903 that the dropping of bombs from the air became a practical proposition. It might be mentioned at this point that the Hague Convention of 1899, a forerunner of the Geneva Convention and meant to govern what armies may and may not do during war, had specifically banned the dropping of bombs from balloons. Such a thing had never been known, but with the research on dirigibles which was being conducted in Europe, it was surely a matter of time before this occurred to some army officer. The Hague Convention was intended to forestall any such development.

Aeroplanes were first used to conduct air raids during the Italo-Turkish War of 1911. Italy felt that they had a claim to territory in Libya, at that time part of the Ottoman Empire. The Italians intended from the beginning that the war in Libya, fought against lightly-armed Turkish troops, should be short and decisive. With this in mind, they sent a considerable force of aircraft, hoping that these would overwhelm the defenders. The Italian Army Aviation Corps landed in Tripoli on 19 October 1911. It consisted of ten officers, twenty-nine men and nine aeroplanes. These were three Nieuports, two Blériots, two Etrich Taubes and two Henri Farmans. Later this initial force was supplemented by some Deperdussins and two dirigibles. In addition to the aeroplanes and troops, there were supporting mechanics and all the necessary equipment to repair any damaged machines.

The first operation conducted by the Italian aeroplanes took place just four days after they had arrived in Libya. Captain Piazza, who was the commander of the air base in Tripoli, took off in a Blériot XI and carried out a reconnaissance flight over the Turkish encampment at Azizia. This was the first time that an aeroplane had been used for aerial reconnaissance in this way and foreshadowed the role of aircraft which would swiftly be adopted during the early part of the First World War, a few years later.

It was only eight years since the first sustained flight by a heavier than air flying machine and so the Etrich Taube monoplane which arrived in Tripoli in October 1911 really was the last word in modern Western technology. The man who piloted the aeroplane, 29-year-old Italian army lieutenant Giulio Gavotti, was to make history of an unsavoury sort. On 1 November, Gavotti took off in the monoplane, carrying a leather satchel which contained four large grenades, each of which weighed about 4lbs. Climbing to 600ft, the Italian flew over the oasis of Jagiura, where he dropped three of the grenades onto Turkish troops camped there. He then flew on to a military camp at Ain Zara, where he threw the final grenade over the side. No casualties were caused by this, the world's first air raid.

Three days later, another air raid was carried out on Ain Zara and the Turks, outraged by what was to them a clear breach of the rules of war to which civilized nations were expected to adhere, protested that the Hague Convention banned the dropping of bombs from the air in this way. The Italians argued that the Hague Convention specified the dropping of bombs from *balloons*. It made no mention of powered, heavier-than-air flying machines. The air campaign in Libya claimed two more 'firsts' the following year.

On 31 March 1912, two Italian airmen were making a bombing raid near Tobruk, when they ran into difficulties. The plane was being piloted by a Lieutenant Rossi, while Captain Montu dropped bombs on the Arab camp below. The Bedouin reacted by firing their rifles up at the aeroplane, which was flying at around 1,800ft. Despite the range, a total of four bullets hit the fuselage of the plane and one of them struck Captain Montu, but he was not seriously wounded. He was the first member of crew on a bombing raid to sustain injury. Lieutenant Moizo, the first pilot to arrive in Libya, flew eighty-two missions between October 1911 and the end of his flying activity in that country in September 1912. On 11 September 1912, Moizo's Nieuport began malfunctioning while he was over enemy territory. He made a forced landing near Azizia and was promptly captured by Turkish forces, the first pilot in the world to be taken prisoner in this way in time of war.

Turkish forces were once again the target of the world's next air raid, which was conducted the following year, this time by the Bulgarians. In 1912, the First Balkan War found Bulgaria fighting against the Ottoman Empire. A two-seater Albatross biplane, which was being used to observe Turkish troop movements, took off on 16 October, piloted by Radul Milkov. His observer, Prodan Tarakchiev, was armed with some custom-made bombs which he dropped on the railway station at Karagac. This can be regarded as the first strategic bombing raid ever recorded. Just as with the Libyan air raid, nobody was killed or injured by this action. The First Balkan War was also notable for being the first in which a pilot was brought down by enemy action. On 3 November 1912, the Reuters' correspondent in Sofia reported that a pilot called Popoff had died when his plane was shot down during a reconnaissance flight over Adrianople. Two other Bulgarian planes were also brought down by gunfire during the First Balkan War. It is interesting to note that the first British pilot to have dropped bombs from the air was Snowdon Hedley, who joined the Bulgarian Army Aviation Corps in 1912 and took part in an air raid on Adrianople.

All the bombing at which we have so far looked was against targets on the ground. Surprisingly, attacks on shipping were also being carried out at roughly the same time, in two different continents. Greece took part in both the First and Second Balkan Wars. In the course of the fighting in 1913, a Farman biplane belonging to the Royal Hellenic Navy was being used for reconnaissance. Flying over Turkish ships anchored in the Dardanelles, the pilot dropped four hand grenades onto them, causing no damage and injuring nobody. At about the same time, on the other side of the world in Mexico, a civil war was raging and an American volunteered his services to General Carranza, whether from idealism or for more mercenary reasons is not known. A Curtiss biplane was dismantled and then brought across the Rio Grande by mule train. The rebels, led by one General Huerta, had a gunboat in the Bay of Guaymas and pilot Didier Masson managed to drop canisters of explosives on it, causing, by his own account, some damage.

This then was the situation as the First World War approached. Aeroplanes were gradually coming to be seen as useful things for an army on campaign, being able to give a bird's eye view of battlefields and spot what the enemy were up to. This was the role which they were to occupy in the opening months of the war. In Britain, they became known as the 'eyes of the army'. It had also been seen that they might have a limited offensive role to play, attacking military targets in support of troops on the ground. It was accepted that their use would most likely be restricted to the battlefield, although the idea had already been mooted that bombing might be used to attack strategic targets far behind the enemy's lines. The first such use had been the bombing of the railway station at Karagac. To use military terminology, aeroplanes would probably be used in a tactical role, which is to say engaging directly with an enemy where the fighting is taking place.

One man who did foresee the possibilities of strategic bombing, as early as 1907, was H.G. Wells. Perhaps because he had previously written books about time machines and an invasion from outer space, *The War in the Air* was treated as just another fantasy when it was published in *The Pall Mall Gazette* in 1908, the year after Wells wrote it. As it happens,

The War in the Air is, along with *The World Set Free*, among the most prophetic of Wells' works.

The War in the Air is, as the title suggests, about aerial warfare. Specifically, the plot features a world war which sees America fighting both Germany and Japan simultaneously, which, considering that it was written 35 years before this actually happened in 1942, is pretty impressive! What is fascinating about the book is that it tells of the bombing of cities by both German Zeppelins and aeroplanes. London is devastated by German bombers, as are other cities. So savage is the war, which ultimately sees the use of biological weapons, that civilization collapses and the world enters a new dark age. This book may be seen as the first iteration of a theme to which Wells returned in *The Shape of Things to Come* in 1933, made into a film by Alexander Korda three years later. In this later work too, air raids and bombing cause the end of civilization, although in *The Shape of Things to Come*, humanity recovers to the extent of being able to embark upon a space programme. We will look in greater detail at both the book and film in Chapter 3.

We have in this chapter traced the idea of aerial bombardment, in both reality and fiction, from ancient times up until the eve of the First World War. This overview has been necessary, so that we are able to see how the catastrophic policy was adopted by both the British and Americans of firing heavy artillery into the skies above their own cities. It is this policy, which amounts to the shelling of their own territory, whose origin we will examine in the next chapter, which deals with defence against air power as developed during the First World War.

Chapter 2

Friendly-Fire Casualties in Britain 1914–1918

The wider causes of the First World War, which began in the summer of 1914, need not concern us here. It is enough for our purposes to know that Britain was fighting alongside Russia and France, against the Ottoman Empire, the Austro-Hungarian Empire and Germany. The *casus belli* which drew Britain into the war is relevant, in that it was directly responsible for the vulnerability of the country to air raids by German bombers. In 1839 Britain had pledged to protect the neutrality of Belgium, a small country between France and the Netherlands. When the German army wished to encircle and besiege Paris in 1914, as they had done during the Franco-Prussian War of 1870–1, it was thought that the best way of accomplishing this end would be to sweep through Belgium. On 3 August 1914, Belgium was invaded by Germany and Britain promptly declared war on Germany. For the next four years, Belgium was occupied by the German armed forces.

Belgium made a far more suitable location for aeroplanes which might be used for strategic bombing raids against the Britain than northern Germany, although this was not the aim of the invasion and it was only later that the significance of the country for this purpose was realized. From Germany, bombers would have to fly for 300 miles across the North Sea to reach the coast of Britain; from Belgium, on the other hand, they would only need to fly 20 miles and once in the air, their destination would be in sight for the whole time. It is no coincidence that the first bomb ever dropped on British soil, on Christmas Eve 1914, landed near Dover Castle. This was little more than a short hop from the airfield in Belgium from which the plane had taken off.

The situation relating to the military use of aeroplanes at the beginning of the First World War may be briefly summarized in this way. They had been found useful in the first instance for carrying out reconnaissance.

An observer, hundreds or thousands of feet in the air, can see far more of what an enemy is up to than can somebody on the ground. They were sometimes called, for this reason, 'the eyes of the army'. Aeroplanes had also been used to drop bombs on both battlefields and strategic targets, that is to say places not on a battlefield but which might help an enemy's war effort, railway lines or factories, for instance. In this sense, they were seen as being like very accurate artillery. Instead of trying to guess where enemy assets might be hidden and then doing one's best to calculate the range and direction of fire needed from the ground, an aeroplane could fly over enemy-held territory, identify targets and then swoop down and drop a bomb right on top of them. This at least was the hope. In practice, things were a little more complicated. To understand why both precision bombing and accurate anti-aircraft fire were so difficult during the First World War, a state of affairs which lasted well into the Second World War, we must examine some simple physics. Unless this is done, we will not be able to make sense of the civilian deaths in Britain which began to occur soon after the bombing of London and other locations by first Zeppelins and later specially designed aeroplanes.

As was quickly discovered in the early days of military aviation, soldiers on the ground were in the habit of firing rifles and machine guns at enemy aircraft and so any bombing mission could not be conducted too close to the ground. To evade small-arms fire, an aeroplane really needed to fly at a height of at least 3,000ft or so. This introduced two difficulties, one for the attacking plane and one for those on the ground hoping to destroy it. If a bomb, or any other object, is dropped from a moving aeroplane, it will not fall straight to the ground and onto the point above which it was dropped. Instead, it will move forward at roughly the same speed as it was travelling when leaving the aeroplane and so strike the earth or sea some distance from the point over which the plane was travelling when the object began to fall.

Let us imagine a slow-moving, by modern standards, aeroplane which is travelling at 100 miles per hour and flying at a height of 3,000ft. When it is directly over the target, a bomb is released. Ignoring air resistance, this means that the bomb will fly forward at 100 miles per hour while also being drawn to the ground by the force of gravity. From that height, it will take about 15 seconds before it reaches the earth. This means that the bomb will strike the ground almost half a mile from the position above which it was dropped, missing the target by a very wide margin. To avoid this error, the pilot will need to know precisely at what speed he is travelling and also his height and position relative to the target. He will then be able to do a few sums and work out at which point he will release the bomb if he hopes to have any chance of hitting the target.

In practice, aiming bombs onto one particular spot when travelling at a great height is all but impossible. One or two real-life examples of the difficulties experienced by the Germans involved in bombing London during the First World War will perhaps make things a little clearer. The first air raid on London by an aeroplane showed the problem which was described above, that of dropping a bomb when one is actually above the intended target. At about midday on 28 November 1916, a single German aeroplane flew up the River Thames and when it was over Central London, at a height of 13,000ft, released six bombs. The bombs were dropped when the plane was right above the Admiralty in Whitehall. Causing explosions at such a hugely symbolic location would have been a great propaganda coup for the Germans. The pilot though had not thought matters through. Because of the factors at which we have just looked, the bombs did not simply drop straight down onto their target. Instead, they kept moving forward at almost a hundred miles an hour as they fell. The result was that they landed not in Whitehall, but around Victoria Station.

Even when careful calculations were carried out by pilots and bomb-aimers, striking a specific building was exceedingly rare. On 13 June 1917 the impressive German Gothas, the world's first specially designed long-range bombers, were deployed against London. A Gotha may be seen in Illustration 6. One intended target was Liverpool Street Station, on the edge of the City of London. This time, although flying at the same height as the plane which dropped the bombs above the Admiralty the previous year, a man with a telescope worked out the correct time to release the plane's cargo. The altitude and speed were known, as was the weight of the projectiles. The bomb-aimer said later:

> With my telescope in one hand, I signal with my other to the pilot. Slowly long rows of streets pass the small orbit of the sight. At last it is time to drop. I give a signal and in less time than it takes to tell, I have pushed the levers and anxiously follow the flight of the released bombs.

The railway station of Liverpool Street is a substantial-enough structure and one might think that with such careful planning, success was assured. In fact, of seventy-two bombs released, only three actually hit the station and one of those failed to explode. Precision bombing from a great height was simply not a practical proposition. All sorts of factors such as the wind were working to cause inaccuracies in the calculations.

The same problem arises when somebody is trying to shoot down an aeroplane. If a man with a First World War rifle, a .303 Lee-Enfield for example, fires at a plane flying 3,000ft above him, which is travelling at 100 miles per hour, then if he is aiming straight at the aeroplane, it will have travelled over 100 feet by the time the bullet arrives. If the aeroplane is travelling at a height of 10,000 or 15,000ft, not at all uncommon at that time, then these margins of error when dropping bombs or trying to shoot anything down will be greatly multiplied. All this is hugely relevant to the methods developed both for bombing and anti-aircraft guns. For bombing, it meant that hitting a specific target such as a railway line or a particular building was all but impossible, unless one was prepared to fly very low indeed and risk being shot down. For those trying to hit aeroplanes as they flew overhead, it became clear that bullets alone were not an effective means of achieving this end. Above 3,000ft, machine guns or rifles were useless, for that is about as high as ammunition at that time would reach, and even lower than that, hitting the aeroplane was a very uncertain business.

One more factor must be mentioned when considering both the accuracy of bombs dropped from an aeroplane and also that of guns firing up at those same aircraft. It is one thing to make careful observations relating to the height and speed of an aeroplane, while still taking into account the strength and direction of the wind, and then carrying out painstaking and meticulous calculations. This sort of thing might be all very well for somebody sitting at a desk in a quiet room. A man aiming bombs being dropped during the First World War though was compelled to work not at a desk, but in an open cockpit at great attitude and in all kinds of weather, such as freezing cold, rain or snow. Many bombing raids took place in the dark as well, which hardly improved matters. When you add to this the explosion around the aeroplane of anti-aircraft shells or attacks from fighter planes, it will readily be appreciated that there might be a tendency on the part of the crew simply to forget about all the sums and just jettison their load and turn for home as soon as possible. This happened not only during the First World War, but in the Second as well. In short, the methods used to deter the bombers had the unintended side effect of making it more likely that they would bomb city streets, which were numerous, than specific military or industrial targets, which were small and often hard to identify.

Of course, similar factors were operating when the crew of an anti-aircraft battery were at work during either of the world wars. Even with all the necessary information about the approaching aircraft, such as their speed and height, the mathematical operation required to turn this information into useful instructions about the time to set the fuze, direction to aim the gun, elevation and so on, are not at all easy. Just as with the crew of a bomber, all this has to be done under all weather conditions, often in the dark and usually under bombardment from the air. Just like the men above them in the sky, there would be a temptation just to blast away after only the most perfunctory calculations and then hope for the best.

One particular aspect of this is very relevant to our investigation into the deaths on the ground from AA fire and that is this. In addition to the fact that many artillery shells in both world wars were defective, those which were being fired at aircraft had to have a time fuze set. In the heat of battle, this fiddly job was one which was often done hurriedly or skipped entirely. This of course increased the chances that the shell would not explode where it was wanted, which was thousands of feet in the air, and would instead plunge to earth and detonate in the street.

The implications of all this were that those dropping bombs from aeroplanes or airships came to realize that they were bound to miss their target more often than not and that their bombs would consequently be unlikely to land where they had been aimed. The same applied to anybody hoping to hit anything thousands of feet overhead; the chances of doing so were negligible. For those wanting to shoot down aeroplanes, a means was needed that would increase the chance of damaging the aeroplane at which one was aiming, other than by being fortunate enough to score a direct hit. The answer was to use artillery shells, which might bring down a plane or Zeppelin if they exploded near enough.

In the previous chapter, we touched upon the fact that hitting anything during a land battle needs just two pieces of information, namely how far away the target is and in what direction. Even if you miss the intended target, you are likely to cause some damage to the enemy army, because you will be firing in his direction. Artillery barrages during the First World War did not need to be all that accurate, because wherever the shells landed, they were inflicting damage on the other side. Things change a little when you are firing almost vertically into the air! In such a case, falling shells or pieces of shells are likely to land on your head or the heads of those nearby, who are most likely to be on your side. Doing this in your own country is almost bound to end with injuries and deaths among your own people.

Another problem when trying to shoot down aeroplanes with artillery is that not only are you now dealing with three coordinates instead of two, but also your target is also moving quickly and often changing both direction and height unpredictably. On land, the enemy is usually in one place, while you are somewhere else. At sea, warships move relatively slowly and so not too much adjustment needs to be made for their positions as they move through the water. Ships of course also move, like targets on land, in two, rather than three dimensions. Aeroplanes though move very fast, travelling at hundreds of miles an hour. Their height changes too. To hit an aeroplane with an artillery shell means knowing how far away from you it is, what direction it is and also how far above the earth. It is also helpful if the aeroplane maintains a steady and reliable speed and height, which is by no means always the case. Not only that, you must be able to calculate where it is likely to be in the future, otherwise, your shell will explode too far away to cause any harm.

Having worked out all this in the middle of a bombing raid, you must then find some way of ensuring that your shell explodes at the right time. There is no point using a shell which will only explode on contact. The chances of that happening are miniscule. The best that one can hope for is that the plane will be a few feet from the explosion and that some fragment of the shell will damage a vital part of the plane. Of course, the more powerful the explosion, the further away will damage be caused. This in turn means that the accuracy of the gun can be less.

All the above factors are of importance when dealing with the bombing by, or the shooting down of, aeroplanes. The first serious bombing raids on Britain were of course carried out not by aeroplanes but by the great airships known, after their inventor, as Zeppelins. It might have been thought that such large, slow-moving and unwieldy craft would be easier to shoot down from the ground than aeroplanes, but this was not really the case. They flew very high and it was only when the British began to use fighters to attack them that the Zeppelin menace was brought to an end.

The use of strategic bombing, attacks on enemy-held territory which do not relate directly to military action currently taking place but rather target the means of industrial production and so on, began almost immediately that the First World War started in August 1914. Of course, aeroplanes were also used at once for reconnaissance, proving to be of crucial importance. At Mons, in Belgium, for instance, the British sent up a plane from which observations were made of German troop movements. This was of inestimable value in preventing the British Expeditionary Force from being taken by surprise. Both the Germans and the British though soon realized that air power could prove decisive in other ways, by attacking the enemy far behind his lines in places where he might otherwise feel safe and secure. On the night of 24 August 1914, with the war only a few days old, a Zeppelin was sent over the Belgian city of Antwerp, where it dropped eight bombs. Also both the French and the British bombed Zeppelin hangers inside Germany, in August and September 1914 respectively.

Once the British and German armies became bogged down in the area which was to become known as the Western Front, the search was on by both sides for a means of breaking the deadlock which did not entail a costly, frontal assault on the fortified positions of the other's forces. The British tried various ways to open up another front, in Turkey and the Middle East for instance. The Germans hit upon the idea of attacking Britain directly by using airships to fly across the ocean and drop bombs on strategic targets. This was the theory, but in practice it proved impossible to distinguish between military and civilian assets, which was to become something of a *leitmotif* in both world wars. An attack on some specific, strategic target inevitably resulted in what the Americans are pleased to call 'collateral damage' to those living and working nearby.

The occasional bomb had been dropped by aeroplanes in the opening months of the war, but the first major air raid on Britain took place on 19 January 1915 and entailed two Zeppelins bombing the Norfolk coast. One of the targets was quite legitimate, the radio station at Hunstanton, but the end result was death and destruction in various villages and towns ranging from Brancaster to King's Lynn. The raid caused no damage to anything other than people's homes and the only casualties were civilian.

Kaiser Wilhelm, the German emperor, had certain scruples about air raids being carried out on London, not least because the British Royal Family were relatives of his, but in the summer of 1915 he authorized the bombing of the docks, providing that no bombs were dropped west of the Tower of London. This pusillanimity did not last though and the capital was soon being bombed anywhere that the Zeppelins could fly over. Since most of the British aeroplanes were being used to prosecute the war in France, it was thought that the best defence against attacks from the air would be to use artillery to try and shoot down the airships now threatening south-east England.

The first anti-aircraft guns used by the British in the defence of their country were the so-called pom-pom guns, which fired a rapid succession of shells, each weighing 1lb (0.5kg). An example of such a gun from the First World War may be seen in Illustration 8. These shells were very light, compared with those of the average artillery piece. As early as 1912, the British set up guns of this kind in the Kent town of Chatham, where the Royal Navy had an important base which they hoped to protect against aerial attack. When the war started in 1914, it did not take long to work out that these small weapons would be quite inadequate for tackling any kind of aircraft at a reasonable height. The decision was accordingly taken to start using heavy artillery in and around British military bases, factories, cities and towns. It was thought that field artillery and naval guns would have sufficient range to reach the Zeppelins, which were flying thousands of feet above Britain.

Other types of guns were also used against aeroplanes and Zeppelins which were bombing Britain at that time. They included French 75mm QF 'auto-cannons' (mounted on trucks) and also 3-pounder British guns. Lighter weapons of this kind were found to be hopelessly inadequate for the job. Even the 12lb (5.4kg) shells fired from the 3in naval guns were too small and later in the war, 16lb (7.2kg) shells were used instead. Obviously, the heavier the shell, then the more powerful the explosion and the greater the range at which damage could be caused and aircraft brought down.

It seemed quite logical during the First World War that the Royal Navy should take the lead in anti-aircraft defence. After all, it was the navy which traditionally defended Britain from attack by foreigners. The army was used abroad, fighting in other people's countries, but it was the navy which defended the country from invasion, by means of warships and coastal artillery. There was of course another and more practical reason that the defence of the country from attack by aeroplanes and airships was entrusted at that time to the navy and that was that the army was stretched to its utmost limit on the Western Front. It was easier to spare a few men of the Royal Navy than it would have been to remove troops from the battlefields of France.

Illustration 9 shows one type of artillery which was used in the early part of the twentieth century to defend the British Isles from attack by hostile, naval vessels. It is a QF 3in gun whose shells each weighed 12lbs (5.4kg). This example is based upon a design which came into service in 1894 and was widely used on ships of the Royal Navy. For firing on a battlefield or at sea, this is an excellent weapon. The one in the photograph is at Tilbury Fort in Essex. Four of these guns were installed at Tilbury in 1903 and guarded the Thames Estuary. The fear at that time was that torpedo boats or armoured cruisers might try to make their way up the Thames to attack London or the Medway towns. This had of course happened in the past, with both French and Dutch vessels.

Firing a 3in naval gun at ships in the Thames Estuary would be the perfect role for guns of this kind. It was close-range work and if the target was missed, then the shell would splash harmlessly into the water. This useful naval gun was the artillery piece which became the favoured anti-aircraft gun of the First World War. Why anybody would think it a good idea to unbolt such a weapon from its concrete emplacement, fix it to the back of a lorry, drive to London with it and then fire it vertically into the air, is an intriguing point.

It was remarked earlier that when you are lobbing shells in the general direction of an enemy on a battlefield, then it is not really a disaster if your aim is a little inaccurate. After all, the shells you fire are sure to do some damage or cause casualties. If nothing else, then they will make the enemy feel vulnerable and tense, which is no bad thing when you are fighting a war. Firing artillery on a battlefield in somebody else's country is one thing. There are no discernible disadvantages to doing this as often as you please. Undertaking the same operation in the middle of your own cities is something else again. It is not easy to explain why anybody would have thought this a wise or desirable course of action and the answer can only be that such a decision was taken as a result of the so-called 'appeal to desperation'.

The appeal to desperation is also known as the politician's syllogism. It runs like this:

> Something must be done.
> This action is something.
> Therefore, this is what must be done.

Nothing else can explain the sheer folly of setting up artillery in centres of population and hoping that using it 14,000 times in 24 hours, as the British did in their own country in 1917, will not have as a natural consequence many casualties among your own civilians. Still, there was no doubt that *something* had to be done. For the first time in a thousand years, a foreign enemy was striking at the heart of the capital. The physical effects of the few bombs dropped from Zeppelins may have been relatively insignificant, but the psychological impact was immense. Governments have fallen for less than this.

There may, in some remote corner of the multiverse beyond our reach and comprehension, exist an alternative world in which the firing of thousands of heavy artillery shells into the skies above one's own cities will not end badly. In our world though, the results of such an action are not difficult to foresee. Apart from any harm caused to airships or aeroplanes, people on the ground will be killed, either by red-hot chunks of metal falling to earth or by shells which explode not in mid-air but when they land in a street or on a house. In short, such a strategy will inevitably result in civilian casualties. How many casualties were caused in Britain during the First World War by shelling the civilian population in this way? Perhaps an expert might give us some idea, somebody like J.B.S. Haldane.

Haldane was a biologist, known for his original work in fields as diverse as statistics and genetics. He is chiefly remembered today for his reply when asked what insights, if any, his studies in biology had given him about the nature of the Creator. He supposedly replied that the Deity displayed 'An inordinate fondness for beetles', due to the enormous variety and sheer number of such insects to be found on the Earth. Haldane fought in the First World War and some years after it ended was invited to join a Cabinet Committee which was investigating the future prospects for aerial warfare, which was an important topic at that time. From 1924 he was a member of the Air Raid Precautions Sub-Committee of the Committee for Imperial Defence. As such, he was privy to a great deal of secret information, so much so that when in 1938 he wrote a book on the subject, his signing of the Official Secrets Act in connection with his previous work in the field, prevented him from exploring some aspects of the topic in detail. Nevertheless, in his book he made several revealing, one might say shocking, statements.

On page 17 of Haldane's book *A.R.P.*, published in 1938 by Victor Gollancz, is a section headed, BRITISH ANTI-AIRCRAFT SHELLS, which contains the following sentence: 'They killed a number of Londoners in 1916–1918. In some raids they caused as many casualties as the enemy bombs.' This is a truly startling admission, that British artillery operating in Britain sometimes killed and injured as many people as the German bombs falling on the country from Zeppelins and aeroplanes. Remember, having served for years on the government committee responsible for examining this very question, Haldane was in the best possible position to know what he was talking about.

As a matter of fact, the situation with civilian deaths from British artillery shells during the First World War was at times even worse than Haldane had said in his book. Perhaps if we look at a fairly typical air raid during that war, we will be able to see precisely who died and the exact causes of their deaths. This is not always possible when hundreds or thousands of people have been killed, but when only a few dozen are involved, it is much easier to establish just what happened. We must bear in mind though that that those writing the history of such events may not always wish to portray the unvarnished truth. This is as true today as it was in the years immediately following the end of both world wars; people don't like to dwell on the blunders which led to British casualties. In the Introduction, we read this account, from a recently published book, of the death of 10 women during the Blitz in 1940:

> Among the major incidents were the deaths of ten Wrens serving with HMS *Daedalus*, RNAS Station, Lee-on-Solent,

> when their hotel received a direct hit during an air raid on 14 September 1940.

Although not explicitly stated, the implication is clear – those ten Wrens died as a result of German bombs. Writing almost 80 years after the event, a modern author is still unable or unwilling to tell the unpalatable truth about an incident of friendly fire. Let us now look at another account, this time concerning the bombing of Britain by German Zeppelins during the First World War. The Wikipedia article on German Strategic Bombing During World War I, https://en.wikipedia.org/wiki/German_strategic_bombing_during_World_War_I#1915, accessed on 15 September 2018, tells us, apropos of a certain type of Zeppelin, that:

> The Army received the first of these, *LZ 38*, and Erich Linnarz commanded it on a raid on Ipswich on 29–30 April and another on Southend on 9–10 May. *LZ 38* also attacked Dover and Ramsgate on 16–17 May, before returning to bomb Southend on 26–27 May. These four raids killed six people and injured six, causing property damage estimated at £16,898.

The source given for this is a standard and authoritative work on the air defence of Great Britain from 1914 to 1918. Similar accounts may be found in many books, internet sites and magazines. We are plainly expected to assume that the six deaths mentioned were caused by enemy action. Let us look in detail at what happened during one of these raids, that on Southend on the evening of Wednesday, 26 May 1915. As readers are aware, Zeppelins were enormous and slow-moving airships.

LZ 38 crossed the Essex coast at about 10:30 that night, having crossed the North Sea. After passing over Clacton, it arrived at the seaside town of Southend at 11:15 and proceeded to drop sixty bombs. Of these, forty-seven were incendiaries and the rest were high explosive. Little damage was caused and few fires started. One boy suffered burns when an incendiary struck his home and a man's wrist was cut after he broke a window in order to rescue his son from a fire caused by another of the incendiaries.

The only real victim of the bombing was a seven-year-old girl called Marion Pateman, who was asleep in her bed when an incendiary bomb crashed through the roof and sprayed burning oil over her bedclothes. The screaming child was rescued by her parents and sister, but succumbed to her injuries two days later, dying in hospital. All things considered, Southend had got off lightly from the sixty bombs, but there was another factor at work, which made things worse. At nearby Shoeburyness, a piece of artillery had been set up to guard the Thames estuary. This gun was used to fire thirty-seven shells up into the air over Southend that night in the vain hope of hitting the Zeppelin. None of them hit their intended target, but the shelling of Southend caused two tragedies.

When artillery shells are fired thousands of feet into the air from one of the 3in guns being used at that time, one of three things can happen. The shell might explode in the air, raining down hot fragments of metal, some of which can be quite sizeable. If the fuze fails to work as hoped, then the shell will fall to earth, where it will either explode on impact or the 12lb mass of steel will crash to the ground at high speed.

One of the shells fired that night from Shoeburyness exploded high above Westcliff, which is a suburb of Southend. William Fairs, a dentist from London, owned a holiday home in Westcliff. His wife and daughter and daughter-in-law were staying at the bungalow, called Fairdene, during the week of the Whitsun holiday. May Fairs, his 35-year-old daughter, had just got off a tram that night when a chunk of metal from an anti-aircraft shell, which had exploded overhead, struck her on the head, killing her instantly. A few streets away, Florence Smith was standing at the front door of her house in Westminster Drive. A shell landed in the road, 30ft from her, and exploded. Pieces of shrapnel scythed through the air, slicing through Florence Smith's breast and cutting her head open. Although for a time it looked as though she might recover from her injuries, Florence died in hospital a fortnight later. This was an unremarkable air raid in which two-thirds of the deaths had been caused not by bombs but by British artillery.

We must, before going any further, make two points clear. The first is that artillery-fire at an object moving thousands of feet above the ground was, before the development of radar and the proximity fuze in the 1930s and 1940s, horribly inaccurate. In September 1940, the first month of the Blitz, the head of Britain's anti-aircraft force estimated that it took 20,000 shells to bring down one German plane. This meant that the tactic developed in the First World War and used also a little over 20 years after that war had ended was to fire as many shells as possible at a target, knowing that the great majority of them would miss. However, the higher the rate of fire, the more likely that by chance alone, one shell might explode near enough to the aeroplane or airship to inflict some damage upon it. This brings us neatly to our second point, which is the confused impression which many people have about the nature of what are usually called 'anti-aircraft guns'.

When we talk of firing 'guns' at targets, we tend instinctively to think of pistols and rifles being aimed at something which is either struck or missed. Of course, if you are firing an air rifle at a row of mechanical ducks in a fairground range, then it really does not matter how often you miss. Nor does it matter in the least if you are firing a shotgun at clay pigeons, whether you hit or miss your target. No harm is done in either case. It is these images which are subconsciously summoned up when people talk of 'anti-aircraft guns', rather than heavy artillery. A moment's thought will of course tell you at once that missing your target above a city when you are using a naval gun firing a shell weighing 80lbs (36.3kg) is likely to have the most serious consequences. This terminology probably lies behind the indisputable fact that few people ever consider the frightful cost in property and lives which the use of anti-aircraft guns wrought in Britain during the two world wars. Experts in the field may talk and write of anti-aircraft artillery, but for the man and woman in the street, they were just 'guns'.

Having cleared up this point, we must bear in mind that we are not talking of 'guns' at all, but rather the kind of artillery used on battlefields to inflict as many casualties as possible when their shells explode. The aim, obviously, is that the shells will only explode near to enemy troops, emplacements, ships or vehicles. On the ground or at sea, this is fairly easy to accomplish, always provided of course that your aim is accurate. A shell can be fired up into the air and will then fall down onto the target, where it will explode on impact. The case is altered when firing at aircraft. Since the odds of actually hitting an aeroplane with one of your shells is vanishingly remote, you must try and get the shell to explode when it is approximately in the vicinity of the aircraft. This was most commonly achieved during both the First and Second World War by setting a timer, a device which caused the shell to detonate at a certain height, in the hope that it would be close enough to an aeroplane to cause serious damage.

There were, during the First World War, two methods used to cause a shell to detonate at a predetermined time. Some work had been done on clockwork timers, but these were not in general use, at least at the beginning of the war. The tried and tested means of getting a shell to explode at a set time was by a gunpowder fuze. These fuzes, known technically as igniferous, worked by a train of powder in the nose of the shell being set alight when it was fired. It would take a certain length of time for this powder train to reach the fuze magazine, whereupon the shell would explode. There were two problems though with using such devices when firing a barrage above your own cities.

Using a train of burning gunpowder to set off an explosion can be a chancy business at the best of times and under ideal conditions. When millions of shells are being produced and used, conditions are not really ideal. Many of them were defective and this meant that they either did not explode at all or exploded at the wrong time. To this day, there are estimated to be many millions of items of unexploded munitions on the site of Western Front of the First World War for this very reason. In the case of shells fitted with a time fuze and used against aeroplanes, the situation was even worse. The speed that a narrow thread of gunpowder will burn had been calculated precisely, but the figures so obtained were only accurate at or near ground-level. Once you ascend a few thousand feet into the air, the temperature drops and the atmosphere is less rich in oxygen. This has implications for the speed at which something will burn.

Shells fired 10,000ft or more into the air often fell back to earth and either exploded or sometimes failed to explode there. This was because of the conditions high in the atmosphere, which had not been taken into account when calibrating the time fuzes. Sometimes the powder train would burn more slowly, at others it would halt entirely, dying down to a glowing ember, before starting again when the shell landed. Gunpowder fuzes are famously unreliable, which of course accounts for the advice given about fireworks which appear to have gone out after the fuze has been lit. One is advised that under no circumstances should you go and examine the firework, because the fuze might splutter into life again, even after a few minutes.

This is perhaps a good place to introduce the commonly used abbreviation for anti-aircraft fire, which is of course AA or, in both world wars,

'Ack Ack'. This latter expression was so widely used that when General Pile, who was in charge of London's anti-aircraft artillery during the Second World War, wrote a book detailing his work in the field, he entitled it *Ack Ack*. The etymology of 'Ack Ack' is a curious one.

Some modern writers claim that 'Ack Ack' is an onomatopoeic phrase, suggestive of the barking of the guns. The smaller-calibre 'Pom-Pom' guns used during the First World War certainly acquired their nickname in this way, from the repetitive sound they made, but this is not the case with 'Ack Ack'. We are most of us today vaguely familiar, if only via fictionalised police dramas on the television, with the NATO phonetic alphabet. This substitutes words for letters, Whiskey, Tango, Foxtrot, for instance, rather than just W, T, F. A single letter spoken over the radio can be misheard, particularly if spoken in an unfamiliar accent, whereas the words 'Foxtrot' or 'Bravo' are less open to misinterpretation.

Although the NATO phonetic alphabet is today in almost universal use, a number of other such systems have been used over the years. Today, 'Alpha' is used in the NATO alphabet to signify the letter 'A', but during the Second World War, the Americans used instead the word 'Able'. One of the oldest of such phonetic alphabets was that devised by the British army in 1904. The first three letters of this system were 'Ack', 'Beer' and 'Cork'. Although a new version was brought in during the First World War, which substituted 'Apple' for 'Ack', the older alphabet was still widely used. This then is the simple origin of 'Ack Ack'; it is no more than 'AA' rendered in an obsolete phonetic alphabet.

It might have been thought that the great airships which were sailing above Britain and dropping bombs in the early years of the First World War would have been as easy to hit with shells as a battleship, but this was not at all the case. Anti-aircraft fire proved very ineffective and it was fighters which finally began to shoot down the Zeppelins, so causing the Germans to abandon their use for bombing. They began instead to use huge aeroplanes. Before seeing how the first serious bombing raids were carried out on Britain by aeroplanes though, a short diversion might prove entertaining.

Firing at them from the ground may have proved in general to be a poor way of tackling the Zeppelin menace, but on one extraordinary occasion, one of the giant airships was brought down not by artillery but by a hail of .303 rifle bullets. Care was taken during the First World War to guard the mouth of the Thames estuary, it being feared that German naval vessels, in particular submarines, might attempt to sneak up the river towards London. A fort at the Essex town of Tilbury had artillery trained on the river as a precautionary measure and eight miles to the west, towards London, were other defences. These consisted of an anti-submarine blockhouse on the edge of Rainham Marshes. Today, these marshes are a nature reserve run by the Royal Society for the Protection of Birds, but during the both world wars, they were used as rifle ranges and for other military purposes.

On the night of 31 March 1916, Zeppelin *L 15*, which was under the command of Kapitänleutnant Joachim Breithaupt, crossed the North Sea with four other airships. The intention was to bomb London. This was at the time when the British had finally concluded that fighter planes were a better means of bringing down Zeppelins than artillery on the ground. *L 15* was damaged by machine-gun fire from just such a plane and turned back over Essex, without reaching London, with the intention of limping home.

The concrete anti-submarine blockhouse on the marshes between Rainham and Purfleet was intended to deal with waterborne craft in the Thames. On the roof was a single Vickers .303 machine gun, which fired the standard rifle ammunition of that time. When he heard that a Zeppelin was approaching from the west, the man in charge of the blockhouse, Captain John Harris, was ill in bed. Nevertheless, he got up, draped a blanket around his shoulders and went out to see what could be done. He ordered the machine gun on top of the blockhouse to fire at the mighty airship and, incredible to relate, the steady stream of bullets worked where artillery shells frequently did not. The gas keeping it aloft began to leak out into the night and *L 15* started losing height. It limped across the Thames, before crashing into the sea on the other side of the river, near Margate. For his achievement, Captain Harris and his men were awarded medals by the Lord Mayor of London. This was the first Zeppelin to be brought down over the British mainland.

The Gotha was the world's first long-range bomber and came into service in early 1917. These twin-engined planes could fly at 15,000ft, carrying 660lbs (300kg) of bombs. After some tentative raids on southern England, the first air raid on London with these aeroplanes was conducted on 13 June 1917. It was a brilliant success. In broad daylight, a formation of fourteen Gothas crossed the Channel from airfields in occupied Belgium and flew to London. Once there, they dropped 118 bombs, killing a total of 162 people. Despite almost 100 fighters taking off to attack them, all the German bombers returned safely to their bases. Illustration 10 shows an ordinary home in London which was all but destroyed by one of the bombs.

If the Zeppelin raids had caused panic, it was as nothing to the reaction of Londoners to this new threat. Prime Minister Lloyd George swiftly took two actions. The first was to bring fighter aircraft from the Western Front to England and assign them to protecting London from this new menace. The second of his actions was a gambit still familiar and much-used today: he ordered an enquiry. The man chosen to head this was General Jan Smuts, formerly a commander in the Boer army during their war against Britain, but now a member of Lloyd George's War Cabinet. Before Smuts had been officially appointed to investigate the bombing of London by German aircraft, another raid took place, also in daylight and with even more aeroplanes, twenty-two this time. We shall look closely at this air raid, because it will shed light upon the subject which we are investigating, the death of civilians as a result of their own army's activities.

On the morning of 7 July 1917, twenty-two German bombers passed over Essex and approached London from the north-east. Anti-aircraft guns opened fire as the raiders split into two groups. One headed to Hendon and the other turned south to fly over Central London. The 2,000 shells which the British artillery hurled into the air did no harm at all to any of the Gothas, but caused havoc on the ground. The bombs dropped by the German planes fell in an arc from Chingford, Tottenham and Edmonton, all the way to the City of London. In all, 44 people were killed and 135 injured by the German bombs. Another ten people were killed and fifty-five injured by falling anti-aircraft shells which exploded in the streets. In short, almost a quarter of the deaths and over a third of the injuries were a result of the British army, rather than the German air force.

Under the headline 'SATURDAY'S RAID OVER LONDON; DANGERS OF THE STREETS', a newspaper at the time reported an inquest into the death of one of those killed by artillery that day:

> The Coroner for North-East London to-day held inquests upon nine persons killed in Saturday's air raid. In the case of

> Simon Percival Noads, 32, export packer, the Coroner said the deceased was struck down near a railway station by a piece of shrapnel apparently from our own guns. It was stated that Noads was in the act of taking cover when he was hit in the chest and wounded in the region of the heart. A verdict of death by misadventure due to his being struck by a piece of shell fired at hostile aircraft was returned.

After bombing London, the German planes turned for home, heading east along the Thames. As a parting shot, they dropped a few remaining bombs on the docks in the Isle of Dogs. These caused no casualties and hardly any damage, other than a barge which was sunk in one of the docks. An anti-aircraft shell though, fired by the British defences, had a defective fuze. It soared thousands of feet into the air and then plummeted down and landed on Strafford Street, in the Millwall district of the Isle of Dogs, where it exploded on impact, killing four people and injuring seven more. They were the only victims of the air raid on the docks that day. All this was bad enough, but it was not the end of the casualties inflicted on their own side that day by the British artillery.

Not a single German aeroplane was hit by the British AA fire. A total of seventy-nine planes of the Royal Flying Corps took off across London and the Home Counties to try and tackle the raiders. One of the bombers was indeed shot down over the Channel, but most of the British planes found that either their guns jammed or that their machines were not powerful enough to climb as high or fly as fast as the Germans. One of these planes, a Sopwith 1½-Strutter belonging to No 37 Squadron, was hit by friendly fire. One of the anti-aircraft shells fired by the ground defences exploded near the plane, bringing it down with the loss of two lives. Both the pilot, 2nd Lieutenant J.E.R. Young, and Air Mechanic C.C. Taylor were killed.

This then was a fairly typical example of a German air raid on Britain during the First World War, over a quarter of the deaths caused not by German bombs, but by British shells. Shocking as this might seem today, when we are familiar only with the bowdlerized version of history which has had removed from it such inconvenient facts, it was widely known during the First World War that the artillery was causing such havoc and death. For it was not only the death toll which was considerable – the shelling of London was also wreaking material damage. During one raid alone, British fire had damaged 300 houses in London, half of them seriously. Londoners were perfectly well aware of what was happening. One man wrote to General Smuts, whose name was associated with the artillery barrage, saying:

> As to your defence of London by this Infernal Barrage I do trust you will stop it, as it is a remedy worse than the disease. We have lived under showers of this odious shrapnel (purely home-made) and it is costly in life and property. A woman close to me was killed in bed thereby.

The woman mentioned in this letter was not the only fatal casualty that week of anti-aircraft fire. At least seven other Londoners had been killed by the same cause.

We seldom hear of this aspect of the defence of London from German bombers, either in the First or Second World Wars. Perhaps when a war is over we prefer to focus on the harm done by the enemy and minimize the injury and death inflicted by our own forces. This was not though how matters presented themselves at the time. Nobody was in any doubt during the air raids on London of the First World War that the use of artillery to defend against the aeroplanes was costly in property and life. Nobody living in the city at that time could have been oblivious to this – the evidence was all around them. On the evening of 25 September 1917, for example, a number of Gothas flew over London, dropping high-explosive bombs. Five people were killed during this air raid and greater or lesser damage caused to over 100 homes and business premises. Anti-aircraft artillery fired 2,690 shells, which partially destroyed 56 houses. One shell landed on a ship moored in the Royal Albert Dock, killing three men.

Another raid, also in September 1917, showed the extent of the danger from the artillery barrages. On the evening of Saturday 29 September, two Gothas and an even larger bomber, known as the 'Giant', flew over London and dropped twenty-six high explosive bombs and one incendiary. The bombs mostly weighed 50kg each and thirteen people were killed during the air raid. In addition to the bombs which fell though, the police in London also recorded that a total of 276 anti-aircraft shells fell on London at the same time. A swift calculation reveals something quite disturbing and unexpected. The total weight of the bombs dropped by the German aeroplanes was at most 1,300kg or 2,860lbs. Assuming that the shells which fell on London were from the 3in guns which were commonly being used at that time, firing a shell weighing 16lbs, means that the total weight of shells which fell on London that evening would have been 4,416lbs, far more explosives than were dropped by the enemy.

The scars from these air raids are incidentally still visible to this day in London. One of the city's landmarks is Cleopatra's Needle, an ancient Egyptian obelisk brought to London in the nineteenth century and erected on the embankment of the Thames. In September 1917 a Gotha dropped its bombs nearby. The stonework nearby is pitted and marked by the force of the explosions and the bronze sphinxes which flank Cleopatra's Needle have jagged holes gouged right through them. Illustration 7 shows some of the damage to a sphinx.

Although this book is primarily concerned with civilian casualties, it may be noted that British fatalities consequent upon anti-aircraft fire were not restricted to the British Isles. Artillery was also being used on the Western Front to try and shoot down German aeroplanes, often those conducting reconnaissance missions over the British lines. At roughly the same time that the two air raids at which we have just looked took place, there was an unfortunate incident near the Belgian village of Wulverghem, where the 5th Battalion of the King's Shropshire Light Infantry were stationed. On 23 September 1917, German planes had been scouting over the battalion's headquarters and attempts were made to discourage them by firing at the aircraft as they flew overhead. One shell failed to explode at the intended height, plummeted back to earth and, as ill luck would have it, sailed straight through the window of a hut at the spot known to the troops as 'Canteen Corner'. There were fourteen men in the hut and two of them, Privates Henry Arthur King and Francis Wilcox, were killed immediately when it exploded in the room in which they were sitting. A total of twelve other men received injuries of varying severity. Just as with friendly-fire casualties in Britain, incidents such as the deaths of the two men at Wulverghem often tended to be lumped in with enemy action, both so the victims could be regarded by their families as heroes and also to avoid embarrassment to the army.

Earlier in this chapter, we looked at the difficulty, indeed near impossibility, of ensuring that dropped bombs fall just where you wish them to land. During the First World War there were a number of terrible tragedies caused by the inherent inaccuracy when bombing from an altitude of 15,000–20,000ft. In June 1917, while bombing the London docks, a perfectly legitimate strategic target, one stray bomb struck Upper North Street School in Poplar. The infants section in the basement of the school was decimated, with eighteen children aged between four and six killed and another forty injured. Civilian deaths of this kind were a feature of air raids in both the First and Second World Wars. Although furious anger was directed against the Germans for such incidents, it is reasonable to place some of the blame for these deaths on the British strategists who thought it a good idea to position heavy artillery in their capital city.

The greatest civilian death tolls occurred of course when poorly-aimed bombs landed on houses, schools and pubs, instead of the military and industrial targets for which they had been intended. Let us carry out another thought experiment. We know that the anti-aircraft guns were useless if considered strictly from the point of view of shooting down aeroplanes. Let us suppose that if, instead of firing thousands of shells at the German aeroplanes, no aggressive action at all had been conducted against them when they flew over British cities. It was largely because they were forced to fly at such great heights, to avoid the AA guns, that the bombs dropped from the aeroplanes went all over the place. If the planes had been able to fly in low and had time to aim carefully and release their bombs from rooftop level, then in all probability no schools or homes would have been destroyed. This goes for both the air raids in the First World War and also the Blitz of 1940. By firing their artillery, the British caused the Germans to fly higher and to release their bombs hurriedly and without time to work out the optimum time to release them.

This seems at first a bizarre and wholly counter-intuitive idea; that the efforts to defend a British city could actually have caused the enemy to inflict more death and destruction than if the armed forces had simply sat patiently and waited for the bombers to carry out their mission. This point will be explored further when we look at the events of the Second World War, because so intense was the barrage of anti-aircraft fire over British cities between 1940 and 1944, that bombers often dropped their loads on the suburbs, rather than run the risk of flying through the flak. In London, this definitely caused far more deaths in the East End than would have been the case without the AA fire.

There was another way that the use of AA fire acted to increase greatly the chances of civilians being killed, either by German bombs or British shells. It was this. Although to begin with the German bombers were making daylight raids on Britain, they soon found, just like the Zeppelins, that it was safer by far to attack at night. This, they hoped, meant that they would be invisible to both the British fighters and also the artillery on the ground. Searchlights were used to probe the skies above London, with the aim of catching the aeroplanes in their glare and illuminating them to the gun crews on the ground. This strategy was also, of course, used during the Second World War. Flying now at night, with the city below blacked out, it was impossible for anybody thousands of feet overhead to make out any target. The most that could be done was to drop the bombs and hope that they found a suitable target. Inevitably, many landed in streets and on schools and public houses.

The statistics for deaths caused by friendly fire in Britain during both the First and Second World Wars are necessarily rough estimates. Even when it is generally known that some death was as likely to have been caused by a British shell as it was a German bomb, there is a natural and wholly understandable tendency on the part of the dead person's next of kin to give their own armed forces the benefit of the doubt and attribute their child's, parent's or spouse's death to enemy action. This at least makes the death somehow noble and means that the person did not die as a consequence of a stupid mistake, but fell as a martyr in the struggle against Nazism or Prussian militarism. An instance of this kind of thing may be seen in Illustration 18. This is the gravestone of a young woman killed in England during the Second World War who, according to the inscription, made 'the supreme sacrifice'.

Here then is how a false view of history has been enshrined in permanent form, to mislead future generations. We shall find out about the story of this grave in a later chapter, but it is enough for now to say that this woman was indeed killed during an air raid, as the inscription on her grave says, but not by a German bomb. She died in January 1944, a month when more people were killed in London by British artillery than by German action. She herself was killed by an artillery shell. Nothing, however, could be more comforting for grieving parents than to persuade themselves that rather than a tragic blunder, their daughter's life was a 'supreme sacrifice', one which elevated her to the level of somebody like Edith Cavell.

We have examined in detail some of the victims of friendly fire in Britain between 1914 and 1918 and it is time now to try and work out a rough minimum figure for the fatal casualties caused during those years by the British artillery which was supposedly protecting them. This will not be easy, for a number of reasons. For one thing, when a bitter war is raging and people are being killed by the enemy on the very streets of your capital city, there is a natural tendency to attribute any injuries or deaths to the foe, rather than the gallant soldiers defending your country. If a piece of metal flies through the air during a bombing raid, the assumption will be that it was a lethal fragment from an enemy bomb. The authorities will be only too happy to go along with this view, however mistaken it might really be. This happened during the First World War, but was particularly a problem during the Second World War, simply because so many more people were being killed and the confusion of war was so much greater.

Because the number of bombs dropped on Britain during the First World War was so much less than in the Second World War, we are able to estimate a little more accurately the proportion killed by bombs, as opposed to the percentage who died at the hand of their own armed forces. The smaller the number of casualties, the easier this is to do. We have seen that in one of the two air raids described above, a third of the deaths were caused by artillery. In the other, two-thirds of the deaths were from this cause. These raids were not exceptional. A simple calculation tells us that the mean average when you add one-third to two-thirds and then divide by two, is one half. If we extrapolate from those two raids, then it might be a reasonable guess that half the deaths during the German raids were from anti-aircraft artillery. This appears to tie in with what J.B.S. Haldane wrote in 1938, that 'In some raids they caused as many casualties as the enemy bombs'.

There are so many imponderables that we cannot be sure of anything in the above calculations, especially after the passage of more than a century. What we can say though with complete assurance is that many civilians were killed by the artillery fired over British cities and towns during the First World War and that at least one expert in the field, a man who had studied the matter in detail, believed that anti-aircraft artillery sometimes posed as great a threat to the lives of civilians being bombed as the bombs themselves did.

The experience of the first large-scale bombing of civilian populations in the First World War shaped the views and opinions of those responsible for defending the country when the next world war broke out, a little over 20 years after the first. In the next chapter we shall see how the theories expounded in the 1920s and 1930s contributed to the civilian death-toll in Britain between 1940 and 1945.

Chapter 3

'The Bomber Will Always Get Through': 1918–1939

The perceived situation at the end of the First World War was very simple. There could be no possible defence against the bomber and it was accordingly hopeless to attempt to deter attack from the air. As early as 1916 Hugh Trenchard, who was to become in 1918 the first head of the newly-formed Royal Air Force, had said, 'The aeroplane is no defence against the aeroplane.' In short, fighters were useless as a means of tackling enemy bombers. It was widely known too that anti-aircraft guns, at least in their present form, were also pointless. During the attacks on London by German aeroplanes, up to 14,000 shells a night had been fired at the bombers without bringing down a single one. The slang name for anti-aircraft fire during the First World War was 'Archie', which said it all. The name was an abbreviation of Archibald and came from the refrain to a popular music hall song, 'Archibald, certainly not!' This was a reference to the fact that the shells never actually hit their intended target.

The only effective, and indeed possible, counter to enemy bombers was to send bombers of your own over the cities of the enemy. If you could be sure to drop more bombs on the enemy's cities than he was able to deliver to yours, and kill more people, then you had won. This was because you might in this way destroy an enemy's means to wage war. In the first instance, this would be accomplished by blowing up his factories and wrecking his railways, roads, ports and docks. Not only would this deprive a nation of the ability to manufacture armaments and transport them to their armed forces, it would also deliver a devastating blow to the morale of the civilian population. Their places of work and homes would be demolished, as would the means to travel to work by buses, trams or railway trains. Without deploying a single soldier on the ground, it should in this way prove possible to win a war by air power alone. Strategic bombing of this sort was seen not so much as an adjunct to conventional warfare, but as a substitute for it. It was suggested that it would be possible to defeat a nation entirely by means of bombing their homeland. No battlefields, no navies, no conventional armies; just pounding the cities from the air until those living there placed so much pressure on their government that peace would be accepted at any price. This notion, that aerial bombardment alone could accomplish what had previously needed large armies and navies, was to become known as the Trenchard Doctrine, after the man who formulated it. Trenchard was quite open and explicit about his belief in this idea, proclaiming in 1921 that 'the next war could be won by bombing alone, by destroying the enemy's will to resist'.

It might be remarked at this point that a version of this doctrine lingered on until a decade or two ago. In both Iraq and Afghanistan, it was thought that with a ferocious aerial bombardment with so-called 'smart bombs', combined with the modern version of the Second World War V1, the cruise missile, a country's ability to go to war might be massively degraded and the population brought to the point of despair. Of course, just as in every war in history, what has now become known as 'boots on the ground' would also be needed, if one wished after the bombing raids to occupy a country, but by the time that infantry were sent in, the people would be so cowed and overawed by the invincible power of the American armed forces that they would not have any inclination to fight. What was explicitly described as a policy of 'shock and awe' by air power would have broken the spirit of resistance. One need only look at the subsequent experience of the American forces in those countries to judge whether or not the will to resist had really been shattered by the display of overwhelming air power.

As the 1920s passed, there grew a mood of increasing pessimism regarding air warfare and its likely consequences for the population of a country under attack. In the same year that Hugh Trenchard suggested that wars could now be won simply by attacking civilians, without the need for all the tiresome paraphernalia of armies and suchlike, an Italian, General Giulio Douhet, published a book called *Command of the Air.* In it, he set out the same basic principles which Trenchard was expounding, that air power alone was now sufficient to win a war.

In America, Brigadier General 'Billy' Mitchell had been appointed Director of Military Aeronautics in 1919. In 1921, the year that Douhet's book was published, Mitchell showed that warships could be sunk by means of bombs delivered by aircraft, using as targets various obsolete American and captured German ships. Few direct hits were made, but the warships were still sent to the bottom of the ocean by the explosive power of 2,000lb bombs.

The destruction of a warship by means of a dropped bomb might have been impressive for a military audience, but in time of war, precision bombing of this kind was to prove an infinitely more tricky enterprise than just flying over a ship and pressing a button! Much more tempting as a target, and a good deal easier to hit, were the homes of factory workers and dockers. These were, almost 20 years before the Blitz on London began, being specifically suggested as the best places for bombers to aim for. In 1923 Major-General J.F.C. Fuller of the British Army explained that in the modern industrial world those labouring to manufacture armaments during a war were as culpable as the soldiers using those weapons. This meant, at least according to Fuller, that 'to attack the civilian workers of a nation will then be as justifiable as to attack its soldiers'. A few years later, Brigadier General Mitchell spelled out just what this meant, by listing some of the most important targets, should there be another war. Instead of airfields, warships or military bases, he wrote of 'The factories, the means of communication, the food producers, even the farms, the fuel and oil supplies, and the places where people live and carry on their lives'. Against the background of such pronouncements by senior officers on both sides of the Atlantic, it can hardly have come as any surprise when, in 1940, both Britain and Germany began bombing each other's cities with little care as to whether their bombs fell on the homes of workers or their places of work.

The projected casualty figures for the bombing of cities in this way were so vast that it seemed impossible even to contemplate any sort of effective civil defence or Air Raid Precautions (ARP). The most that could be hoped for was to maintain the morale of those living in cities long enough to give your own bombers time to bring about the collapse of the enemy's country. This became, for the British, an official policy. Bombing of strategic targets such as factories and railway lines was all well and good, but the primary purpose of such attacks was, at least according to the RAF, the effect of the bombing on civilians. In the *RAF War Manual*, published in 1935, we find the following:

> Moral effect – Although the bombardment of suitable objectives should result in considerable material damage and loss, the most important and far-reaching effect of air bombardment is its moral effect

In Parliament, British politicians were determined to emphasise both that bombing of Britain would be very dreadful and also that there was no way of preventing it or mitigating its effects. In 1932, Prime Minister Stanley Baldwin famously told the House of Commons that it was important:

> For the man in the street to realize, there is no power on earth that can protect him from bombing, whatever people may tell him. The bomber will always get through . . .

Since the bomber would always get through and no power on earth could protect its targets, it followed as a matter of common sense that spending money on anti-aircraft guns was wasteful and unnecessary. It is, incidentally, interesting to see what else Baldwin said in that same speech. Everybody remembers that most memorable of soundbites, 'the bomber will always get through', but what is less well-known is that at the same time, the British Prime Minister set out quite bluntly the likely progress of any future European war in which Britain were to become embroiled. He continued: 'The only defence is in offence, which means that you have to kill more women and children more quickly than the enemy if you want to save yourselves.' A couple of years later, Winston Churchill reminded the House how grim things were likely to get: 'We must expect that under pressure of continuous air attacks upon London at least three or four million people would be driven out into the open country.'

Churchill went on to paint a vivid picture of the pressure which this vast mass of refugees, without food, water or shelter, would place upon the government. There were, it must be said, excellent grounds in the mid-1930s for the pessimism being exhibited by leading politicians, including the Prime Minister himself, on the prospect of any country defending itself from an assault by waves of bombers. The RAF had been carrying out various exercises in the years following the end of the First World War and the results of these were very far from promising, when it came to defending the country from attack.

In 1926 the RAF tested their ability to shoot down an approaching aeroplane by using anti-aircraft guns. In the last chapter we saw that anti-aircraft fire had proved hopelessly ineffective during the First World War, but there were those in the RAF who believed that it might be feasible to develop a robust system of defence using artillery. The results of this test were even worse than anybody could have anticipated. Even when the target was flying at a constant speed and known height, by trailing a sleeve target from behind an aeroplane, at which the artillery would aim, only two shells in 3,000 struck the target. And this was under ideal conditions, with clear weather and an obliging pilot who did not take evasive action to avoid the guns. It even proved difficult to hit stationary targets.

Another exercise in 1932, the year that Stanley Baldwin warned the House of Commons that the bomber would always get through, seemed to confirm his gloomy prophecy. The RAF used hundreds of aircraft and the idea was to see if fighters were capable of intercepting bombers and preventing them from reaching London. The results of the exercise were that although some of the supposed bombers were intercepted and adjudged to have been shot down, most got through. As many as 20 per cent of the bombers could be stopped by fighters, but the great majority were not. Losses for the defenders were heavy and the message for both military leaders and politicians seemed to be that Stanley Baldwin was quite right and that the bomber would always get through.

Fortunately, there were those who did not give up entirely on preparing for the defence of the country against air raids. While the standard and accepted view might well have been that the only way of defending the country was to build a bigger fleet of bombers than any other European country possessed, others were still looking for some method to increase the effectiveness of air defence by means of fighters. This work led to the development of what was then called Radio Direction Finding, which we know today as radar.

In the 1930s and early 1940s, warning of the approach of enemy aeroplanes was, it was hoped, to be provided by a series of 'sound mirrors' which were aimed towards Europe. Construction of this acoustic early warning system began during the First World War and continued up to the 1930s. Gigantic parabolic dishes were built from concrete and the idea was that the drone of distant bombers approaching Britain would be picked up and magnified by these structures. An operator with a stethoscope sat at the focal point of each mirror, listening carefully. If he heard anything alarming, then the ordinary telephone system was used to alert an airfield and fighters were scrambled. The only real drawback to this peculiar, Heath-Robinsonesque system was that it did not work. In 1934, a test of one of the sound mirrors was disrupted in the morning by the passing of a milk float. A visit was expected later that day from Air Marshal Dowding, who played such a crucial role a few years later in the Battle of Britain. The milkman was asked not to return in the afternoon, lest his vehicle should disrupt a demonstration of the early-warning system which was to be made for Dowding's benefit!

It was the awfully ineffective and unreliable sound mirrors which were generally used to help the aim of anti-aircraft guns during the Blitz, which might account in part for the notorious inability of the AA guns actually to hit any enemy aircraft. In Chapter 10 we shall see how the acoustic mirrors were superseded by radar and the 1930s saw the establishment of a line of radar towers known as Chain Home. These gave Britain a distinct edge in the Battle of Britain, although they were less useful during the Blitz which followed.

Using projected figures provided by the Air Staff, the Ministry of Health decided in 1938 that in the first few months of a war, around 600,000 people would be killed by bombing. They too feared a complete collapse of society under the burden of such casualties. The prospect seemed unremittingly bleak for Britain if another European war broke out.

While soldiers, scientists and politicians were carrying out their careful calculations, other influences were at work, some of them entirely fictional. There are uncanny similarities here between the way that nuclear weapons were regarded in the 1950s and how they found their way into speculative books and films. There was a widespread assumption after the devastation caused to the Japanese cities Hiroshima and Nagasaki became generally known, that any future war would end in either the total destruction of the world or, failing that, the death of most of the population, with a handful of survivors struggling to cope with a new dark age following the collapse of civilization. This theme was explored in novels such as John Wyndham's *The Chrysalids*, published in 1955, and *On the Beach* by Nevil Shute, published in 1957 and made into a film two years later. Novels, short stories and films depicting a post-apocalyptic world contributed during the 1960s to the rise of the Campaign for Nuclear Disarmament (CND) and a pessimistic view of the long-term prospects for the human race. Such attitudes affected in turn the outlook of politicians and planning for the eventuality of war. Exactly the same thing happened in the 1930s, with the fear of a world devastated by the bomber leading to the formation of the Peace Pledge Union.

In 1936 a film called *Things to Come* was released. A collaboration between Alexander Korda and H.G. Wells, it was an adaptation of Wells' 1933 novel, *The Shape of Things to Come.* Some of the scenes in the film were disturbingly prophetic. Massed formations of bombers were shown flying over the white cliffs of Dover and dropping their loads upon a city which was clearly meant to be London. Anti-aircraft guns fired ineffectually at the aeroplanes overhead, which reduced the city to ruins and killed most of the inhabitants. The year of this aerial attack was given as 1940. The war dragged on for decades and ended with scenes of the former citizens of London eking out a living in a society which appeared to be comparable to that of the medieval period.

In America too, fictional accounts of a desolate planet in the aftermath of a ruinous world war were also being published. On 31 July 1937, *The Saturday Evening Post* published a short story entitled *The Place of the Gods.* This story, which has since been republished many times under the title of *By the Waters of Babylon*, tells of a primitive society living in America in the distant future. Their culture is about the level of the ancient Egyptians and they live by scavenging from the ruins of an older civilization which was brought down by a terrible disaster. The protagonist undertakes a journey to the ruins of a great city, which we later learn is New York. There, he has a vision and discovers that those who once lived in the city were destroyed by 'fire from the sky' and a 'deadly mist'. Since this was written eight years before the explosion of the first atomic bomb, the end of New York and American civilization can only have been brought about by conventional bombing, combined perhaps with poison gas.

Stephen Vincent Benét wrote *The Place of the Gods* as a reaction to the bombing of the Basque town of Guernica during the Spanish Civil

War, the same event which inspired Picasso to produce perhaps his most famous painting, which he named after the ravaged town. This too is relevant to British attitudes to defence against attack from the air, because during the 1930s the principles of the new kind of warfare which had been set out from the end of the First World War onwards were seen in practice in a European country and viewed as a harbinger of things to come.

The Japanese were of course bombing civilians in China, as were the Italians in Abyssinia, but these were far-away places in other continents. Spain, however, was only a short distance from Britain and the activities of the German air force there, in support of the Nationalist side in the civil war, was seen in newsreels shown at cinemas across the whole of the United Kingdom. The destruction of the city of Guernica in particular was widely regarded as a portent of what modern war was like.

Germany helped the Nationalist forces of General Franco to win the Spanish Civil War and it was thought by many people that they relished the opportunity to field-test some of their latest weaponry. Whether or not this was true, the effects of modern methods of warfare on Guernica, which were reported across the world, together with the bombing, again by German aircraft, of the Catalan city of Barcelona, reinforced the despair with which the average person contemplated the prospect of air raids. The aftermath of the German air raids on Barcelona were filmed for Pathé newsreels and seen by all cinema-goers in Britain. There were regularly other clips of film on the newsreels, showing German Stukas dive-bombing. The overall impression was that the orthodox view was the correct one and that there could be no defence against bombers.

The news from Spain was more than a little misleading. A Spanish market town in a district unprotected by fighter planes might very well be devastated by a few air raids, but this could hardly be compared to the situation if an attack on London were to be mounted. There was another, fundamental message from the bombing of Republican-held cities and towns in Spain, although most people missed this aspect of events in that country. It was this. Even if the bombers *did* get through, their effect might not be quite as disastrous as many of the experts predicted. Hand-in-hand with the notion of the bombers always getting through went the idea that this would lead to the complete demoralization of the civilian population, mass flight from cities, madness, hysteria, riots and uncontrollable civil disorder. It was upon this scenario that most of the

British Air Raid Precautions had for some years been predicated. Despite the terrible destruction and deaths of many civilians in the Republican parts of Spain, nothing of the sort happened. Quite the opposite in fact. One contemporary writer noted that:

> Observers state that one of the most remarkable effects of the bombing of open towns in Government Spain had been the welding together into a formidable fighting force of groups of political factions who were previously at each other's throats.

In other words, the bombing had acted to unify, rather than fragment, society.

As the Second World War was about to begin in 1939, the position in Britain was as follows. The majority view was still that there could be no defence against enemy bombers, whose arrival might signal the collapse of society. The aim of defence, according to these prophets of doom, should be to pour all the country's resources into setting up a bigger force of bombers than anybody else and to use them to attack the homeland of anybody who started bombing Britain. A fairly substantial minority of politicians and military figures thought this attitude to be muddle-headed and wrong. They believed that building more fighters and developing early-warning systems would enable Britain to hold its own against an attack and perhaps fight off the bombers.

The two factions described briefly above both shared one opinion though about the best means of shielding Britain from attack. They both knew without the shadow of a doubt that anti-aircraft guns were a waste of time and unlikely to affect matters one way or another, at least as far as deterring or tackling bombers was concerned. For that reason, the anti-aircraft artillery defences which had been in place at the end of the First World War had been largely dismantled. What guns there were had been transferred to military and industrial sites. The reason was simple. Experience in the First World War had shown that such weapons posed a far greater threat to the civilians of one's own side than they did to enemy aircraft. Nobody really thought in terms of using guns to defend against air raids.

It was all well and good for military theorists to discard heavy artillery as an appropriate method of countering enemy aircraft flying over one's territory, but such a view fails to take into account one important fact about artillery. It is noisy and obtrusive. People can hear and see it. They can also feel its effects as the earth shudders during a barrage. The real defences which Britain was constructing during the late 1930s, things such as the chain of radar towers which would provide early warning of the approach of aeroplanes from Europe, were of course top secret at that time. People who are under attack want to be able to see what steps are being taken to protect them. Steel masts a hundred miles away on the Kent coast will not be enough to reassure a Londoner who sees bombers flying overhead and dropping explosives on his district. Seeing fighters firing at the enemy's planes might do the trick, but of course when one is being bombed at night, which was the case for most of the Blitz, it is hard to distinguish between your aeroplanes and those of the enemy.

The one thing which might serve to demonstrate to ordinary people that their government is taking serious steps to fight back against the devils who are dropping bombs on their homes is some very visible action – firing heavy artillery nearby, for example. Before we actually find out in detail what went on in Britain during the Second World War, we have to realize that the use of artillery in and around cities was by public demand. Everybody who knew anything at all about the matter was aware that it was pointless and hazardous, but it was what ordinary people wanted. This does not of course exculpate those who took the decision to launch artillery barrages above crowded cities from the lethal consequences of their decision.

Chapter 4

The Outbreak of War, 1939

At the outbreak of war in 1939, two main ideas or themes influenced official attitudes towards the possible aerial bombardment of Britain's cities, although the gloomy outlook engendered by the attitudes which had held sway for so long had been ameliorated in the last couple of years by some hasty attempts at rearmament and the building of defences. The only way to defend cities was by following that well-known dictum of the Prussian military theorist, Carl von Clausewitz, the one which holds that the best form of defence is attack. In other words, striking back at the bombers overhead by means of fighter planes or anti-aircraft guns was hopeless. The only sensible response to the dropping of bombs on your own country would be to attack the enemy by bombing his homeland, inflicting more damage than that being done to your own cities. Despite this widely-held view, the development of fighters such as the Hurricane and Spitfire had of course been hurried through in the 1930s and thankfully Britain would not be left completely at the mercy of the Luftwaffe.

A natural corollary of the belief about the bombers inevitably getting through defences was the acceptance that anti-aircraft fire was utterly unable to prevent incoming bombers from reaching their targets. In addition to this, it was known from the experience of the First World War that anti-aircraft guns were not only useless as a deterrent to bombers, but represented a greater threat to the civilian population than they did to the crews of enemy aircraft. From a strictly military perspective, anti-aircraft guns were quite useless.

The second major strand in the British government's thinking on this matter related to Air Raid Precautions (ARP). Because, no matter what actions were taken, the bombers were sure to arrive in the skies above Britain and there would inevitably be many casualties, little could be done about the injuries and deaths that would be caused. The projected death rates from bombing raids were grotesquely exaggerated in the years immediately before the outbreak of war in 1939, which made the whole idea of reducing or mitigating casualties seem hopeless. The practical aim of ARP would accordingly be directed not towards preserving life, which was impossible, but rather at maintaining the morale of city-dwellers and preventing their flight into the countryside, thus bringing about the consequent collapse of the nation's industrial capacity to wage war. Anything which strengthened morale and encouraged the population to remain at their posts in factories was to be encouraged. The death toll was to be regarded as regrettable, but inevitable. The important point was that a much higher death toll should be exacted upon the enemy's civilian population.

Again, in the same way that a belated realization that fighters might actually come in handy if war broke out, so too had a policy of providing air-raid shelters been embarked upon. This was being done partly through the distribution of the corrugated-iron Anderson shelters for people's back gardens and also by the building of public shelters.

Despite the gradual change in perception and attempts to prepare some defences against bombers, it was thought far more important to stockpile cardboard coffins, commandeer swimming pools as makeshift mortuaries and to recruit team of psychiatrists to deal with the many cases of madness which would be sure to result from the bombing of Britain's cities. After all, the projected death toll for even the first few weeks of bombing ran into hundreds of thousands and that most eminent of thinkers, Bertrand Russell, had declared that once the bombing began, then, 'London will become one vast raving bedlam, the hospitals will be stormed, traffic will cease, the homeless will cry out for peace . . .'

In fact, during the first year of war, the lives of people living in Britain's cities were far more at risk from the measures taken by their leaders than they were from the military actions of the country's enemies. Before we look at the death toll exacted on the civilian population by both German bombs and British artillery, it might be interesting to see how hundreds of people a month were dying as a direct consequence of the dreadful fear of the bomber getting through. Although not strictly 'friendly fire' casualties, these many victims certainly died through the actions of the British government and have largely been forgotten as thoroughly and comprehensively as the men, women and children who were blown to bits by their own armed forces.

Within half an hour of the Prime Minister's sombre announcement on 3 September 1939 that, 'this country is at war with Germany', air-raid sirens sounded in London, presumably signalling an imminent attack by German bombers. This was the moment when all the theories of modern warfare would be put to the test. It had been carefully calculated that each ton of bombs dropped on a city would kill seventy-two people. A force consisting of 200 bombers, each dropping around a ton of bombs, could therefore be expected to kill 14,400 Londoners in a matter of hours. In the event, it was to prove a false alarm, but despite not appearing in the skies above British cities for another year or so, the bombers, or rather the fear of the bombers, still managed to exact a dreadful toll.

During the Zeppelin and Gotha raids of the First World War, limited blackouts had been imposed in London. These were only a pale foreshadowing of the real thing, which was to be rigorously instituted 48 hours before the declaration of war in September 1939. The cry of 'Put that light out!' is of course a familiar one to many people who were not even born when the Second World War began. It was immortalised by Bill Pertwee, playing the part of ARP Warden Hodges in the popular television sitcom, *Dad's Army.* For anybody living in Britain between 1939 and 1945, there was nothing in the least comical or amusing about the blackout. At best, it was a constant nuisance, at worst it was a deadly hazard.

Every window of every building, not only in cities, but everywhere else, had to be covered in material which prevented even a chink of light from showing. Cars had to drive without lights, there were no streetlamps, and even striking a match to light a cigarette out of doors was frowned upon. It was actually a criminal offence under the blackout regulations to display a lit cigarette during an air raid. More than one hapless smoker was accused of signalling to the enemy by this means. There were two practical consequences of the blackout. One we shall look at shortly. First though, we must consider the immediate effect of plunging the country into darkness. We begin with the first British casualty of the Second World War, a man of whose name few are likely to have heard; Police Constable George Rodney Southworth.

The blackout was instituted a couple of days before the declaration of war, and strictly enforced on the Sunday evening of the day that Neville Chamberlain made his famous speech to the nation, informing them that their country was now at war. It took a little while for everybody to adhere strictly to the new requirements and, as usual, some people were a little more officious and keen to enforce regulations than others. One such person was 25-year-old PC Southworth, who was, on the day following the declaration of war, patrolling London's West End, between Regent's Park and Oxford Street. As he walked along Harley Street after dusk, he noticed a light showing in a fourth-floor window. Unable to persuade anybody to answer his determined knocking on the front door, Southworth decided to climb up the outside of the building, get in through the window and extinguish the light himself.

Gripping his electric torch between his teeth, PC Southworth began to climb up a drainpipe. From there, he was able to get onto a ledge on the first floor, which gave him access to another pipe. In this precarious fashion, in complete darkness apart from the light of his torch, the young police officer succeeded in reaching the third floor. It was there that disaster struck, for he lost his hold upon the pipe and plummeted down to the street below. He died of his injuries a short while later. This tragic accident was the first recorded death in Britain to occur as a direct result of the Second World War.

Police Constable Southworth might have been the first person to die because of the blackout, but he certainly wasn't the last. The lack of any kind of artificial light at night made the streets horribly dangerous for pedestrians. There were all sorts of accidents, from tripping over the kerb to falling in canals, but the greatest risk was that posed by motor vehicles. It had been thought especially important that cars, buses and trams showed no lights, because otherwise the roads of Britain would have been clearly and obviously delineated from the air by strings of glowing beads of light. For people crossing the road though, the new situation was a nightmare. Little wonder that the Ministry of Transport did not at first wish to publish the figures for road traffic accidents after the blackout was instituted. We know them now though and shocking reading they make too.

The last four months of 1939 saw a 100 per cent increase in deaths on the road in Britain, as compared with the figure for the same period in the previous year. The great majority of those killed were pedestrians. The increase in fatalities was not evenly distributed across the whole country. In Glasgow, for instance, three times as many people were killed in the closing months of 1939. Wilfred Trotter, the King's surgeon, wrote to the *British Medical Journal* and observed that 'by frightening the nation into blackout regulations, the Luftwaffe has been able to kill 600 British citizens a month without ever taking to the air'. A survey carried out in January 1940 found that one person in five claimed to have suffered injury of some kind because of the blackout. In Parliament, Winston Churchill complained at the strictness of the British regulations compared with other European countries which were nominally at war with Germany. In France, lights were still visible and the traffic was not mowing down anything like the number of people being killed in Britain.

From a purely practical perspective of saving lives, the blackout was a waste of time. By the time the Blitz began in September 1940, thousands of lives had already been lost due to the darkness. Like the anti-aircraft guns though, it gave the citizens of big cities a boost in their morale. It was hugely unpopular, but like some nasty-tasting medicine, it was generally assumed that it must be doing some good! People were almost lynched for showing lights at night and even the lighting of a cigarette in a doorway could result in an offender being reported to the police and fined. People believed that the blackout was good for them and protected them from danger. In fact, the complete opposite was true; for the man and woman in the street, the blackout greatly increased their chance of dying both by being run over by a motor car and also being blown up during a bombing raid. It is not difficult to see why.

Finding and correctly identifying a city such as Coventry or Canterbury might well prove challenging in complete darkness, if you lack any assistance from radio beams. This is not at all the case with London, as Neville Chamberlain saw, a year before the Second World War started. He was returning by plane from the conference in Munich in 1938 and, as the aeroplane in which he was flying followed the course of the River Thames west from Southend, Chamberlain reflected on the horrible idea that German bombers could one day follow this same route to the capital. He was quite right. of course. Even on the most overcast and moonless night, the Thames glitters beneath one, leading straight to the heart of London. As long as you can find the Thames estuary, which stretches between the Kent and Essex coasts, it is child's play to navigate your way to London.

The Luftwaffe was not greatly affected by the blackout, because once a few of their planes had found their way to London, it was not difficult to show others the way. Zealous and overbearing ARP wardens and police officers might have been able to badger and bully their neighbours into painting their windows black or avoiding lighting their pipe in the garden at night, but they were unable to prevent German aircraft from dropping incendiaries during daylight raids, which started raging fires lasting until long after dark and thus furnishing the city with its own beacon to attract the bombers carrying their cargoes of high-explosive bombs. Once the pathfinders had found London and set parts of it on fire, the whole blackout was rendered utterly pointless. The government and army knew this perfectly well. They were aware, for example, that the bombers were, even without any lights below to guide them, using the Isle of Dogs and Hyde Park as handy reference points, flying to those two places and then taking bearings from there before heading off to their actual targets.

In the next chapter, we shall see the role that anti-aircraft fire played in causing civilian casualties, but the blackout too was responsible for some of the deaths during bombing. To understand why, let us carry out another thought experiment. Imagine for a moment that it is 1940 and that there is no blackout operating in London. The German bombers fly over the city and select their targets carefully. They wish primarily to attack sites of strategic importance, docks, factories, airfields and so on. Because the city and surrounding areas are brilliantly illuminated, the pilots and bomb-aimers have no difficulty in doing so. They are readily able to identify the ordnance factory in Enfield, the Woolwich Arsenal, the docks on the Isle of Dogs and anywhere else that they wish to destroy. Because everything is so lit up, there will not be too much problem about finding these places and depositing their bombs upon them. Probably some houses will be struck in the process, but such collateral damage will be rare.

Now let us contrast this with the actual situation when the Luftwaffe flew over London in 1940. They might find London itself easily, but trying to locate some factory or other in the darkness will be extremely tricky. The bombers will not wish to return to base with their loads and so they will most likely jettison the bombs in the general area of the target for which they are seeking. This will mean the bombs landing in the streets around the factories and docks, which will inevitably have the effect of making the death rate soar. Looked at in this way, not only has the blackout brought about thousands of deaths from accidents, it has also precipitated indiscriminate death and destruction in the capital. London is full of streets of houses and dotted here and there are sites of military or industrial importance. If a bomber is compelled, because of the blackout, to drop its load randomly, then there is of course statistically a far higher chance of those bombs landing on homes, rather than ordnance factories.

This increase in civilian deaths was the actual intention of the blackout, however it may have been presented to the public. The destruction of a factory making aeroplanes or tanks will harm a country's ability to wage war far more severely than the blowing up of a row of houses and death of those living in them. If we take it for granted that the British government expected enemy bombers to be flying over the country and hoping to attack strategic targets, which we may take as a given, and that the aim of the blackout was to conceal these assets from sight, then it follows quite logically that it must have been realized that the bombers would end up dropping their bombs far less accurately, because of the blackout. All this seems quite obvious. It follows then inexorably that the government preferred to see bombs landing on the streets surrounding armament factories and so on, rather than the bomb-aimers being able to see the targets and hit them. It must therefore have been known that the blackout would increase the number of casualties during an air raid, the object of the exercise had nothing to do with protecting the civilian population.

Before looking at what actually happened during the Blitz, which we shall do in the next chapter, this might be a good point at which to pause and see how the Blitz fits into the largely fictional history which the British have constructed about the Second World War. The distorted version of events in Europe which is the standard story of the years between 1940 and 1945 is important for Britain, among other reasons, because it provides justification for the British and American attacks on German cities. These were ten times worse than the harm caused to London and other British cities by German bombing but, like a playground dispute, the received account of the war allows us to claim of Germany that 'He started it!' It is upon the claim that Germany began the bombing of cities, together with the number of casualties caused in this country by the bombing, that the British absolution from having committed war crimes by their own bombing campaign depends. There are many who regard the British fire-bombing of Hamburg and Dresden as war crimes, but if it is true that the Germans started the bombing of defenceless civilians, then that might make the actions of the RAF slightly less dreadful. It is of course not true though, that it was the Germans who began the bombing of cities and that Britain was merely retaliating.

The accepted British narrative of the early years of the Second World War runs something like this. In 1939 Germany invaded Poland and, as a result, Britain declared war on Germany. This was in September 1939 and for the next six months or so, nothing much happened, the period which became known as the 'Phoney War'. Then, in April 1940, Germany attacked, and soon conquered, Norway and Denmark. The following month came the invasion of Belgium and the Netherlands, followed by the Fall of France and the evacuation from Dunkirk. Britain now stood alone against the might of Nazi Germany. Before Hitler could deal with Britain as he had those other countries which his army had subjugated, it was necessary to break the fighting power of the RAF. There followed, in the summer of 1940, the Battle of Britain. When it became obvious that this strategy was failing, the Germans turned to the bombing of British cities, starting with the Blitz on London. Britain could take it and years later, revenged themselves upon Germany for the Blitz by treating Berlin, Dresden and Hamburg in precisely the same way.

This account is a very satisfying one, in that it shows Britain as David standing against Goliath and then later triumphing in spite of insurmountable odds and dishing out the same medicine to Germany as it had inflicted upon Britain. So deeply entrenched in the British psyche is this mythic narrative that it may seem literally incredible to many people that the whole thing is no more than a fairy story. We shall be looking in the next chapter at whose explosives actually killed the victims of German bombing raids on Britain, but first we need to consider whose fault it was that there was any bombing at all of British cities. To do so, we must return to the day that Germany began the invasion of France, which was 10 May 1940.

Apart from Germany's attack on Western Europe, another other important event took place on 10 May 1940. This was the collapse of Neville Chamberlain's premiership and the appointment of Winston Churchill as a leader of national unity, able to command the support of not only the Conservatives but also the Labour Party at a time of unprecedented crisis. No sooner had Churchill become Prime Minister than he ordered the bombing of a German town. The day after he became Prime Minister and four months before the German air force launched the Blitz against London, thirty-six British bombers struck at the German town of München-Gladbach, now known as Mönchengladbach. Only four people were killed in the city centre, but the raid set in motion a dangerous chain of events, which was to culminate months later in the German bombing of Britain. Ironically, one of those killed by British bombs in München-Gladbach on 11 May 1940 was an Englishwoman.

Since the subject of this book is civilian casualties of friendly fire during the Second World War, this seems a good point at which to mention that the impact of the British raid on München-Gladbach was amplified by the fact that it was the second air raid on Germany that day. The first had occurred when a squadron of bombers flew over the town of Freiburg-in-Breisgau and dropped several tons of bombs on it. A total of fifty-seven people were killed, including thirteen children in a school playground. The people in the town quite naturally assumed that they were being bombed by either the British or French, but it later transpired by the aeroplanes were German and due to a navigational error had bombed their own country, under the impression that they were over the French town of Dijon.

Five days after the bombing of München-Gladbach, the RAF staged the first hundred-bomber raid on Germany. Well, almost a hundred; in fact on the night of 15 May, ninety-nine bombers set off to bomb targets in the Ruhr. Two days later, on 17 May, an even bigger air raid was made on various German cities. That night, 135 British planes bombed, among other locations, the centre of Hamburg, where 34 people were killed.

That four months before the Blitz, Britain was sending over large forces of bombers to attack German cities is not something generally known to the British public, even today, 80 years later. It makes a nonsense of the whole accepted story of the bombing of Britain when we discover that it was the British who began bombing cities and that the Germans did not retaliate in kind for months. The simple fact that it was Churchill who gave the order for bombing raids against German cities, long before the beginning of the Blitz, has two consequences. First, it shifts responsibility for the British deaths in the Blitz away from Germany and towards Britain. Since the British began the killing of civilians in this way, we can hardly blame Germany for fighting back in a similar fashion. Secondly, it removes the justification for the later actions of the British in the war, when they bombed to destruction cities such as Hamburg and Dresden. The firestorm which engulfed Hamburg in 1943 is often shrugged off on the grounds that it was no more than Germany deserved after they had razed Coventry to the ground three years earlier. If it was the British themselves who first began the game of bombing each other's population centres, then the case is altered.

It is time now to look at what actually happened during the Blitz on London and other British cities and the real cause of the tens of thousands of deaths which occurred during the air raids by the Luftwaffe. The role of the anti-aircraft guns which were deployed in a number of cities will be crucial in our understanding of the events of 1940 and 1941 and this will be the subject of the next chapter.

Chapter 5

The Blitz, 1940–1941

The sporadic bombing attacks on Britain, both on land and at sea, continued throughout much of the 'Phoney War', intensifying greatly after the Fall of France and the British evacuation of Dunkirk. The German aim at this point was strictly strategic, to gain mastery of the air over Britain and the English Channel so that an invasion fleet could be launched, carrying troops to occupy Britain. Obviously, such a seaborne armada would be at greatest risk from attack by the RAF during the crossing of the Channel and so it was vital that the British air force be rendered harmless. It is for this reason that the major assault by the Luftwaffe, when it came in August, was launched not against the civilian population but rather against the British air force. Airfields and, to a lesser extent, radar stations were the chief targets of the German bombers. Some cities were hit by German bombs, but these were aimed at specific strategic locations such as factories.

The first thing to become abundantly clear was the anti-aircraft guns protecting factories and airfields from attack from the air were more or less useless. It was the fighters which were able to combat bombers. This struggle for mastery above Britain and the English Channel was called by Churchill at the time, 'the Battle of Britain'. He said, on 17 June 1940, 'What General Weygand called the battle of France is over. I expect that the battle of Britain is about to begin.' The expression captured the public imagination and has ever since then been used to describe the aerial combat between the fighters of the RAF and the aircraft of the Luftwaffe.

There are many myths about the Battle of Britain, but this is not really the place fully to explore these. There is, for instance, the strange idea that the RAF pilots were all British officers. In fact, fewer than half of them were. Roughly a fifth were foreigners, including over 150 Poles, and a third were non-commissioned officers – sergeants or flight sergeants. The imbalance of forces between the British and German air forces was nowhere near as great as was later suggested, either. Whatever the details though, the RAF fought back hard against the Luftwaffe, although by the first week in September they had almost run out of aeroplanes and men to fly them. In those seven days, the RAF lost no fewer than 161 aircraft. It was at this point, when just a little more effort on the part of the Germans might have finished the RAF as a fighting force to be feared, that a miracle occurred. The relentless attacks on the airfields came to an abrupt halt, giving the British air force a chance to recover a little.

Just how close the RAF came to being defeated by the Luftwaffe can be seen by the situation eight days after the bombing of London began. At that time, although the Germans were also attacking civilian targets, they had not quite despaired of fatally weakening the RAF and so clearing the way for the invasion of Britain. On Sunday, 15 September 1940, Winston Churchill sensed that matters had reached a climax and went in person to the Operations Room of No. 11 Group in Uxbridge, on the outskirts of London. He there witnessed the turning point in the Battle of Britain, which would decide whether or not the Germans launched their invasion.

Air Vice-Marshal Keith Park was directing the fighters above south-east England and sent three more squadrons into the air. The Prime Minister was uneasy, fearing that not enough forces were being held in reserve. Churchill wrote after the war about the scene:

> Hitherto I had watched in silence. I now asked, 'What other reserves have we?'
> 'There are none.' said Air Vice-Marshal Park.

It really was that desperate a situation: every aeroplane was in the air and fighting. Fortunately, at this crucial juncture, just as the RAF were on the very cusp of defeat, the Luftwaffe gave up their attacks on military targets entirely and instead widened and expanded their operations against cities. This gave the RAF the chance to regroup and recover a little from the onslaught.

Just what brought about this vital breathing space has been a matter of some debate. There are many possible explanations, one of which has become the definitive one which appears in most history books. There is another though which, if true, would indicate one of the most wickedly cynical actions ever taken by a British government. Let us deal first with the widely accepted course of events. According to this, the Luftwaffe was scrupulously careful to stick to military and strategic targets in Britain, all through the 'Phoney War' and the Battle of Britain. Then, on 24 August 1940, a group of bombers aiming for aircraft factories in Kingston-upon-Thames somehow became hopelessly lost and inadvertently dropped their bombs instead on the centre of London. Furious at this attack on the civilian population, Churchill ordered a reprisal raid against Berlin. Hitler, infuriated in turn by seeing his own capital city being bombed, then ordered the Blitz against London. If only Churchill and Hitler had been a little more level-headed, it could all have been avoided.

The problem with the above account is that it is, to be charitable, a gross distortion of history. Put a little more bluntly, it is a pack of fairy tales. The first civilian in the British Isles to be killed by the Luftwaffe had died five months earlier. James Isbister, a 27-year-old road labourer living in the Orkney Islands, had been the victim of a German bombing raid on the British fleet, which was lying at anchor in Scapa Flow. In the confusion of the attack, both high-explosive bombs and incendiaries were dropped on a village in the parish of Stennes on 16 March 1940. A number of houses were damaged, but James Isbister was the only fatality. Three-and-a-half months later, on 1 July, the Scottish town of Wick was bombed, killing fifteen people. Among the dead were seven children, ranging in age from five to nine. Nine days later, the English and Welsh towns of Falmouth and Swansea were bombed, resulting in the deaths of thirty civilians.

Of course, by the time the Luftwaffe had done all this, the RAF had already been killing civilians in Germany throughout May. It is fruitless to enquire as to whether the targets in these attacks by the German and British air forces were actually military: the fact is that civilians were being killed by bombing in both countries for six months before the Blitz began. On 17 August, a week before the German bombers supposedly lost their way and accidently triggered the Blitz, a secret survey was carried out in Britain of all casualties up to that time. It was found that 729 civilians had already been killed by the Luftwaffe.

The final nail in the coffin in the traditional sequence of events which led to the Blitz began is provided by the fact that Churchill did not order the bombing of civilians in Berlin at all. The RAF raid was aimed at armaments factories to the north of the city. There was low cloud and this confused some of the pilots, who went off course and dropped their bombs in the centre of Berlin. This was hardly a provocative act: Germany and Britain had been bombing each other's cities for months at that point.

There is another possible explanation for how the Blitz began and the Germans switched from largely attacking military targets and began concentrating instead on trying to kill as many civilians as possible. It has been suggested that the bombing attacks on German cities, which as we saw began three months before the Battle of Britain, were an attempt to provoke Germany into the sort of counter-city strikes which Britain had been preparing for during the 1920s and 1930s. By this reading of the situation, the bombing of Hamburg and other cities, months before the beginning of the Blitz on London, were carried out with the express hope that Hitler would order the Luftwaffe to retaliate and that the kind of war of attrition which most military experts had though likely would then be initiated. If true, this would mean that the Blitz suited British strategy, by allowing civilians to be killed, rather than the military structure of Britain to be degraded by air attacks. This was, after all, the type of war for which the British had been preparing since the end of the First World War, striking with bombing at enemy cities, rather than engaging the enemy in the air.

Whatever the true explanation, at about 5.00 pm on Saturday, 7 September 1940, 375 German aeroplanes flew to London in broad daylight and began dropping bombs, chiefly on the docks and surrounding areas. Inevitably, many of the bombs fell on residential streets. In addition to the high-explosive bombs, incendiaries were also used to great effect. For an hour, both types of bomb rained down on the East End of London. Then, the raiders left as swiftly as they had arrived, leaving a large part of East London ablaze. The Blitz had begun.

This might be a good point at which to mention that the term 'Blitz' is a horribly inapt way to describe the war of attrition which was waged between Britain and Germany between the autumn of 1940 and early summer of 1941. The origin of the expression is interesting. The memory of the ghastly stalemate of trench warfare that led to the slaughter of so many young lives on the Western Front during the First World War was a potent one in both Britain and Germany. In Britain, it led to the rise of a pacifist movement and encouraged appeasement. Anything was thought to be better than another European war. In Germany though, thoughts turned to another means of avoiding the horror of the trenches and this was to be achieved not by renouncing war, but rather by ensuring that when it came, it could be won quickly.

In 1937 Heinz Guderian, who became a general in the Wehrmacht during the Second World War, published *Achtung-Panzer*, outlining a new theory of modern warfare. Fast-moving armoured columns, supported by air attacks, would punch holes through enemy lines and then race to the rear, disrupting communications and supply lines. The essence of these new tactics would be the speed with which an attack would be undertaken. Two years after the publication of *Achtung-Panzer* came the invasion of Poland. The speedy conquest of the country, following Guderian's doctrine, became known by the portmanteau word of Blitzkrieg or 'lightning war'.

The attack on Britain in September 1940 was not at all the same kind of war which had resulted in the Nazi conquest of Poland, Norway, Denmark, France, Holland and Belgium in a matter of months. No fast-moving tanks would be accompanying the bombing of cities, nor would mechanized infantry or airborne troops be taking advantage of the aerial bombardment. This was to be a slow process, rather than a lightning-quick one, the Blitz would continue for eight months, hardly a lightning-war. Still, the name stuck and so today, 80 years later, we still remember this bombing campaign as the Blitz.

In the last chapter, we saw that the blackout had been causing many deaths and a great deal of inconvenience to the people of Britain, long before the Luftwaffe appeared overhead. A few hours after that first air raid on London, the London docks were blazing so fiercely that the glow could be seen 30 miles away. When darkness fell, the Luftwaffe returned and pounded the East End again with a further 330 tons of bombs and many more incendiaries. The blackout was thus proved to be quite pointless. While people had been fussing about an unshaded lightbulb or somebody lighting a cigarette without shielding the lit match from sight, a huge bonfire had been created which could be seen from the English Channel.

The bombing raid on London which took place on 7 September 1940 became known as 'Black Saturday'. The reaction of the authorities to this new German tactic, one which both sides had, after all, been thinking about for many years, was to greatly increase the death toll among the civilians of Britain's cities and towns.

So sudden and wholly unexpected had been the attack on London that it was not until half an hour after the appearance of the German aeroplanes that any of the anti-aircraft guns fired at the raiders. There was some excuse for their hesitation, because RAF fighters were weaving among the bombers, trying to disrupt their formation and shoot down the planes before they could wreak havoc on the streets below. This was not an easy task, because the bombers were accompanied by a strong fighter escort. At the end of the day, thirty-three German planes had been brought down for the loss of twenty-eight British fighters.

On Sunday, the Luftwaffe returned to London, as they would almost every night for the next eight months. After the first few days, they realized that the RAF were not, as they had been led to believe, a spent force, but rather a very real and present danger during the hours of daylight. For this reason, bombing at night became the usual practice. The RAF had a few night fighters fitted with an experimental version of airborne radar, but these were not sufficient, at least in the early days, to make any real impact on the forces of bombers. It was upon the ground-based forces that the British began to rely for defence, with disastrous consequences.

From 'Black Saturday' until Tuesday, 10 September, the anti-aircraft guns in and around the capital were under strict instructions to fire only when they had identified a target and had a reasonable chance of hitting it. These instructions were complicated, and rendered almost unworkable, by the presence of British fighters darting among the German planes. Nobody wished to take the chance of anti-aircraft fire bringing down one of their own planes, as had actually happened a year earlier at the so-called 'Battle of Barking Creek' on 6 September 1939. On that occasion, just three days after Britain had declared war on Germany, a misinterpretation of data from one of the radar towers of Chain Home on the east coast led to fighters being scrambled from two airbases, North Weald and Hornchurch. When the Hurricanes from

North Weald encountered the Spitfires from Hornchurch, both sides thought that they were seeing German aircraft, with the result that they engaged in a dogfight over East London.

The fighting between the two groups of British aeroplanes a few days after the start of the war ended with the first death of a British fighter pilot in action during the Second World War, when Pilot Officer Montague Hulton-Harrop's Hurricane was shot down by a Spitfire from Hornchurch. While the Spitfires and Hurricanes were battling it out, anti-aircraft artillery on the ground opened up, bringing down a Spitfire. It was this incident which led to the strict rules of engagement which discouraged the AA guns in London from firing at the German raiders during the opening days of the Blitz. Nevertheless, they did fire when they had a clearly identifiable target, although without killing any Germans.

On the Sunday after 'Black Saturday', one gun crew had unobstructed views of Luftwaffe planes and felt that they were justified in firing at them. This was done and although all the exploding shells failed to harm the Germans, one of their shells was defective and instead of exploding in the air, fell to earth near King's Cross Railway Station in Central London. It landed outside a crowded café, killing seventeen people. Because few bombs had fallen in the area, it was at once obvious what had caused the casualties, although this terrible instance of friendly fire was not advertised. It was a harbinger of things to come.

On Monday and Tuesday, the bombers returned. It became clear that the bombing of London was going to become a daily occurrence. On 'Black Saturday' it was not until half an hour after the first bombs had fallen on London that any anti-aircraft guns responded. Even when they did begin firing, it was a desultory and half-hearted effort. No planes were shot down and in some parts of the capital, around the East End for example, no guns at all could be heard. After a few days of intensive bombing from the air and an almost complete lack of retaliatory action from the forces on the ground, it began to appear to many ordinary people as though the government simply did not care about their plight, that there was no political will to respond to the bombing and defend them from the enemy.

The whole aim of Air Raid Precautions was the maintenance of public morale, and nothing more injurious to morale can be imagined than the feeling that one's family has been abandoned by the powers that be and that you and your neighbours are regarded as merely cannon fodder. This was how those cowering in shelters began to feel during the first few nights of bombing, that no orders had been given to fight back and deter the German bombers. One of the canons of Westminster Abbey, F.R. Barry, had picked up very quickly on this dangerous mood and made it his business to contact the Prime Minister directly, by approaching Churchill's parliamentary private secretary Brendan Bracken, and telling him that, 'If this were allowed to go on there would be anti-war demonstrations which the government might not be able to contain.' Feelings were running very high about the lack of any visible and violent response to the bombers flying over London. Violet Regen, sheltering in East London, summed up the mood: 'Apart from a solitary salvo loosed at the beginning of the raids, no gun had been shot in our defence – and morale was by now pretty low.'

Low morale was of course precisely what the government was most anxious to prevent at any cost. On the afternoon of Sunday, 8 September, 24 hours after the bombing of the docks and East London had begun, Winston Churchill visited some of the bombed areas and was enthusiastically received. Witnesses agreed that he had been greeted with cries of, 'We can take it, but give it 'em back!' Churchill promised, 'repayment with compound interest'. Although the Prime Minister was almost certainly thinking of the strikes which he would make against German cities in retaliation, the people of the East End wanted to be able to see and hear British forces in action, to assure them that some effort was being made to protect them.

The preparations which had been made by the British for the expected bombing of London by Germany had all been based on the assumption that hundreds of thousands of people would be killed and that those not killed outright would be driven mad by the slaughter and probably attempt to flee into the countryside. Provision had been made for such eventualities. Thousands of cardboard coffins had been stockpiled, teams of psychiatrists were on standby to deal with the outbreaks of mass neurosis and madness, and army units were ready to cope with the flood of refugees. The one thing which might perhaps have benefited those whose homes had been bombed though, had been neglected. There were hardly any air-raid shelters. It is true that since the previous year,

Anderson shelters had been distributed to those who wanted them. These were for use in gardens though, needing to be dug deep into the ground and have earth piled upon them to be effective as a means of sheltering from explosions and falling shrapnel. Most of the cramped, terraced houses in the streets of Poplar and West Ham lacked gardens, of course. The only recourse of those living in such districts was to go to public shelters. These were shoddily-built brick structures which, being above ground, were vulnerable to blast. It was never envisaged that large numbers of people would be spending night after night in these places and they lacked sanitary provision and basic amenities.

After the first few days of the Blitz it was plain that something would have to be done to reassure Londoners that their government cared about them and was committed to preserving their lives. This was a particularly delicate situation, since it was the poorer, working-class districts of East London which bore the brunt of those first raids. Member of Parliament Harold Nicolson kept a diary during the Second World War, in which he recorded a conversation with Clement Davies, an MP who was to become leader of the Liberal Party for over a decade after the end of the war. Nicolson had already noted that, 'Everybody is worried about the feeling in the East End, where there is much bitterness'. A short while later, after the Luftwaffe had begun dropping bombs on other parts of London, such as the West End, Nicolson wrote that Clement Davies told him that, 'if only the Germans had had the sense not to bomb west of London Bridge there might have been a revolution in this country. As it is, they have smashed about Bond Street and Park Lane and readjusted the balance.' Fortunately for the stability of the nation, the German air force soon expanded their field of operations to include the smarter parts of London, such as the West End. This explains the Queen's often-quoted remark after Buckingham Palace was bombed on 13 September. She said, 'I am glad we've been bombed. It makes me feel I can look the East End in the face.'

RAF night fighters were operating in the skies above London, but they succeeded in shooting down few enemy planes. In any case, this sort of attack on the German bombers was not especially noticeable to the men and women huddled in Anderson shelters. Something a little more obvious was needed. Members of the British government thus found themselves in a dreadful bind. If they followed their natural inclination and pursued the course of action which the Trenchard Doctrine demanded, then they would continue to accept that the bombers were unstoppable and the only sensible way to respond was to counter-attack by striking at Germany's cities. Follow down that road though and it would look to the general population as though their leaders had no regard for them and did not care if they lived or died. This could easily lead to the very thing which the authorities above all feared – a complete collapse of morale, widespread panic and wholesale flight from the cities to the relative safety of the countryside. What, though, was the alternative?

Winston Churchill, in whose hands the ultimate decision rested, had of course during the First World War inveighed against the folly of using anti-aircraft guns to defend London in precisely similar circumstances, correctly describing anti-aircraft guns at that time as 'instruments of self-bombardment'. His most trusted scientific adviser, Professor Frederick Lindemann, showed by the most careful calculations that aiming at and shooting down a single bomber by means of the technology being employed by the anti-aircraft batteries was almost inconceivably unlikely. To have even one chance in fifty of bringing down a bomber travelling at 250 miles per hour, it would be necessary to fire 3,000 shells every second at it! Even General Pile, in overall command of the capital's anti-aircraft guns, knew that as a means of countering German bombers, his guns were useless. After the end of the war, Pile said that in September 1940 it was necessary to fire 20,000 shells in order to destroy one bomber. Despite all this, the decision was taken massively to increase the rate of fire against the bombers. Not, it was readily conceded by all concerned, because this would cause any particular harm to the Germans, but simply to generate enough noise to be heard across the whole of London, thus furnishing the illusion to the citizens that something was being done to protect them. In short, it was decided to kill a number of Londoners by means of artillery fire, in order that those who were not killed should have their morale boosted and so be discouraged from fleeing the city.

This raises a most interesting philosophical and ethical point. The increasingly strident demands for artillery fire on London were coming from the very people who would most likely fall victim to the shells. Of course, they did not know that the chances of any of those shells actually bringing down any of the German bombers was vanishingly small. Nor did those calling for action properly realize that there would be a far greater risk that they themselves would be killed by the guns than that any Germans would die in the attack. The government though was perfectly well aware of both these facts.

Although everybody involved knew that it was a pointless enterprise from a military point of view, anti-aircraft artillery was removed from where it had been protecting military and industrial targets and rushed to London, until by the evening of Tuesday, 10 September, there were twice as many guns in the capital as there had been on 'Black Saturday'. At a meeting on Tuesday evening, General Pile announced that from the following day every gun was to fire continuously, without worrying about aiming at any target. The fighters of the RAF were to be wholly withdrawn, leaving only enemy aircraft in the skies above London. The main thing was to hurl as many shells into the sky as possible, creating as much noise as could be in the process. Abandoning the pretence of aimed fire did not really make any difference. The AA guns had at their disposal just eleven gunlaying radar units, which could estimate the height of an aeroplane to within a few hundred feet. All the other guns were still reliant upon the sound mirrors which had begun to be erected at the end of the First World War. These might have been some use if the bombers approaching London had been so obliging as to flight in straight lines, at a steady speed and without varying their altitude at all. Few did so. On Wednesday evening, every piece of artillery in London fired continuously over an area of about 200 square miles. In all, over 13,000 shells were fired. Not a single aeroplane was hit.

We shall at this point conduct yet another thought experiment and see exactly what the consequences of the cynical decision to shell London really amounted to in practice. We begin by considering what would happen if a single German bomber were left, unmolested, to carry out its mission to bomb a strategic target in London. Let us take a typical bomber which might have been found in the skies above London in September 1940, a Dornier Do 17. This bomber, nicknamed because of its slim profile the 'flying pencil', had proved its worth in Spain, when it was used to support General Franco's forces during the Civil War. It had a range of 750 miles and carried a bomb-load of 2,200lbs (1,000kg), just a few pounds short of an Imperial ton. Unopposed, the Dornier 17 would have flown to London, dropped 2,200lbs of bombs on factories, docks or military positions and then returned to Germany. It is unlikely under such circumstances that many civilians would have been killed: the bombs would not have been deliberately dropped on residential areas. We shall now consider how different the situation might have been had this same Dornier been shot down by British artillery.

There are many imponderables, but let us make some rough calculations about the effect of anti-aircraft fire in London in September 1940. To shoot down that Dornier would have taken at least 20,000 artillery shells to be fired above London, according to the man who was in overall charge of the AA guns in and around the capital. Some modern writers claim a figure of 30,000, but let us try and be as conservative as possible in our estimates and work with the figure provided by General Pile, who had no reason to exaggerate the shortcomings of his artillery. The next thing to work out will be how heavy those shells were and how likely they were to explode on the ground, rather than in the air. Various different types of artillery were being used in London during the early part of the war. Some naval guns had a calibre of 4.5in and their shells weighed 55lbs (25kg). In addition to these were the 3.7in anti-aircraft guns, firing 28lb (12.7kg) shells and also the much small Bofors guns whose shells weighed a mere 2lbs each. Looking at Illustrations 12 and 13, we see two gun turrets from warships, which had been removed from the ships and placed in on Clapham Common in South London and Wanstead Flats in the east. These are QF 4.5in naval guns and they were hurling shells weighing 55lbs into the air continuously throughout the Blitz. Illustration 15 shows a pair of Bofors guns, mounted on a warship.

Most of the guns being used in London were heavy artillery. The Bofors guns were more useful for defending airfields against dive-bombers, rather than against heavy bombers at a great height. We shall assume that the average weight of the shells being fired at the beginning of September 1940 was 30lbs (13.6kg). This figure is probably a little on the low side, but our aim is to work out a minimum figure for the damage inflicted by the British on their own side by a policy of wholesale and indiscriminate firing of artillery over and onto their own cities.

The next question to consider is what percentage of the shells fired would explode in the air and how many would hit the ground and explode there instead. This is a trickier calculation. We know that the clockwork time-delay fuzes being used were not as efficient as those which had previously been imported from Switzerland. We know too that many of the men setting those fuzes and firing the guns were not of very great ability. General Pile himself called them, 'the leavings of the army intake'. There were a lot of Home Guards too. One person working on the proximity fuze which was being developed during the Second World War mentioned in passing that 'half the shells fired exploded on the ground'. This may be an exaggeration. Another estimate is that 5 per cent did not explode until they landed. We shall use a number between these two extremes and assume that 10 per cent of the shells fired either had defective fuzes or that the fuzes had not been set correctly. In the next chapter, we shall see how easily this can happen under fire, when American sailors in ships in Pearl Harbor inadvertently bombarded Honolulu.

We are now in a position to make a very rough estimate of the actual effects of authorizing the large-scale use of artillery in London in the opening days of the Blitz. To prevent that lone Dornier Do 17 from dropping 2,200lb of bombs on a strategic target in London, it would be necessary to fire 20,000 artillery shells at it. Around 10 per cent, that is to say 2,000 of those shells, might have fallen to the ground and exploded in the streets of the capital. If each weighed an average of 30lb, that that means that a total of 60,000lb (27,215kg) of shells would have exploded on the streets of London, which equates to the explosive force delivered by twenty-seven fully laden Dornier bombers which drop their bombs. So far, we have hardly improved matters for the people of London. Is that the worst of it? By no means.

Apart from the shells which would have exploded on the ground in London, another 18,000 would either have exploded in the air or crashed back to the ground unexploded. This meant a rain of perhaps 200,000 chunks of red-hot metal falling across a wide area, killing people and damaging property. It is worth mentioning that even a shell which did not explode at all could still kill civilians. We remember too the advice contained in the 1939 government publication *Air Raid Warnings* that 'most of the injuries in an air raid are caused not by direct hits by bombs but by flying fragments of debris or by bits of shells'. Look again at Illustration 3, which shows a chunk of metal weighing a pound or so and which would, by the time it reached the ground, be travelling at perhaps 200 miles per hour. Just try and imagine what 200,000 pieces of shrapnel like that would do to those on the streets. Actually, we don't need to imagine, because there is no shortage of accounts of people killed by such shell fragments. Here is one such. In *The War on Our Doorstep*, an account of the effects of the Blitz on the East End, the author of the book, Harriet Salisbury, quotes Violet Kentsbeer regarding one unexploded shell:

> It wasn't a bomb that injured my family, it was the shells from the guns in the park. They didn't explode, they just came down in the middle of the road, and the shrapnel, it was only small pieces, but it hit them right in their groins as they were standing in the porch, ready to go on their duty, firewatching.

Violet Kentsbeer's sister was killed in this incident.

Then too, there is the small matter of a large aeroplane falling to earth. We are all of us, since 11 September 2001, aware of the danger to human life of an aeroplane crashing into the middle of a crowded city. One final point which needs to be borne in mind is that all those exploding anti-aircraft shells would have the inevitable effect of making the bombers fly much higher than would otherwise have been the case. This means that their bombs were more likely to strike away from the designated target. Indeed, there is some anecdotal evidence to suggest that German bombers approaching London and seeing the barrage of exploding shells simply dropped their loads at once, on whatever suburb they happened to be passing over, and turned for home.

Comparing the likely outcome of a bomber simply being left to fly to its target and drop its bombs with the likely outcome if it was instead shot down, has been massively counter-intuitive. Our common sense tells us that of course it would be prudent to stop a bomber from striking one of our cities if humanly possible, especially our capital city. However, we have seen that such a course of action would be at least twenty-seven times as bad for the people on the ground as leaving that bomber to its own devices, a surprising discovery indeed! Even if the figures we have used are hopelessly wrong and we halve the number of shells which exploded when they hit the ground, this would still leave us with thirteen times as much explosive power being expended on the ground as would have been delivered by the plane which had been shot down.

There can be little doubt that Churchill, Pike and most of the others involved in authorizing the firing of every anti-aircraft gun in London on

Wednesday, 11 September 1940, must have known perfectly well that the orders which they were giving would result in the death of hundreds or thousands of Londoners. Balanced against the crucial factor of increasing the morale of civilians and stiffening their resolve to stay put in the capital, this was not a major consideration though. In effect, the British army was shelling London to prevent its citizens from fleeing from the city.

From Wednesday onwards, every anti-aircraft gun in London opened fire continuously, as long as ammunition was to be had. There was no question of waiting until a target was identified, that didn't matter. The only important thing was to make as much noise as possible and let everybody know that the guns were firing at the enemy. It didn't even matter if this ceaseless activity damaged the guns or rendered them inoperable. At one point, the barrage was so intense that the barrels of the artillery pieces were beginning to overheat, which could prove ruinous. General Pile ordered that some guns be rested and organized a rota, so that some guns were firing while others were allowed to cool down. Churchill, when he heard about this, ordered it to stop. He told Pile that the guns could rest when there were no more German bombers over London.

To the man and woman in the street, the sound of the artillery was delightful. It meant that they were now hitting back and the pounding of the guns drowned out the sound of the exploding German bombs. It certainly acted, as Churchill hoped it would, as a morale-booster. Writing after the end of the war, he was quite candid about what the artillery did and did not achieve:

> This roaring cannonade did not do much harm to the enemy, but gave enormous satisfaction to the population. Everyone was cheered by the feeling that we were hitting back . . .

The reaction of those cowering in shelters was all that could be desired. It was what Churchill had called the, 'roaring cannonade' that they wanted. Diaries and newspapers of the time all emphasize the noise created by the guns, without mentioning at all any aeroplanes which might have been shot down. Barbara Nixon, who was an air-raid warden, wrote that, 'on Wednesday they brought up the guns at last. There never was such an exhilarating uproar . . . It was a splendid and deafening cacophony.' The next day's *Daily Express* hit the nail on the head when they described, 'gunfire louder than the bombs'. This is what people wanted, for the sound of the British guns to drown out the noise of the exploding bombs. Incredibly, artillery was moved about London and fired in many different places, just so that people could hear the guns.

Writing many years after the war, Geoffrey Taylor, a police officer in H Division during the Blitz, described how guns were taken up and down the East End, so that everybody could hear them at work. He said:

> After a week of incessant aerial bombardment Winston Churchill moved into London all the guns that could be spared, and though I did not see any planes hit, it was gratifying to hear the noise and it cheered up the people who had been clamouring for action.
>
> One really large gun used to travel up and down a railway line near the Garage and made quite a din.

Guns were also mounted on lorries and driven about the streets. These parked outside public shelters and fired off a few shells, just so that those inside would hear that something was being done to hit back at the Germans.

The wild artillery barrage, which was to continue for the next eight months, was greeted with universal acclaim. The noise not only drowned out the sound of the aeroplanes and falling bombs, it served to reassure the people of London that something was being done to protect them. Home Office reports over the next few days said that the main feeling of ordinary people was expressed by the claim that, 'We'll give them hell now!' Nobody seemed to have noticed that no aeroplanes were actually be shot down and because of the hundreds of deaths and great destruction of property, nobody had noticed either that the artillery was killing innocent people rather than German pilots.

Some readers may be a little puzzled about the idea of artillery shells landing in the streets of London during the Blitz and there might even be a suspicion that the whole thing is being, if not actually made up, at least greatly exaggerated. Such a feeling is quite understandable, because the history of the Home Front during the Second World War has been carefully crafted and cunningly honed to erase all mention of the matter. When bombs are falling on a city and explosions are taking place everywhere, there is a natural tendency to lay the blame for any deaths or destruction at the door of the enemy, rather than those trying to protect you. This is no more than human nature. It explains why, in a book quoted in the Introduction, one which was published as late as 2017, a particularly shocking instance of the carnage wrought by a British shell is attributed instead to a German bomb. In a moment, we shall look in detail at that case.

Before seeing the kind of thing which not uncommonly happened during the Blitz on Britain, we recall that there are perfect examples of how dangerous it could be to fire artillery near your own cities in the experience of the Americans in 1941 and 1942. On two occasions, American artillery fired at targets above their own territory, with unfortunate consequences. During the Japanese strike on Pearl Harbor in 1941, for instance, the American naval guns killed more of their own citizens than they did enemy attackers. In the next chapter, will shall be able to look at how Second World War artillery could wreak havoc when being used near cities under combat conditions. For now though, we return to the Blitz on London and other British cities. Even those commanding the anti-aircraft guns described their actions as, 'wild and undisciplined firing'. Let us look at one or two specific incidents in the days after the AA guns in London were given the go-ahead to fire at any or no targets.

We have chiefly been concerned so far with the loss of human life caused by artillery in Britain, but there was also extensive damage to property. So used are we to seeing pictures of the devastation caused by the Blitz and assuming as a matter of course that this was a consequence of German bombing, that it may come as a something of a surprise to learn that some of the first damage caused to London landmarks such as Westminster Abbey and No 10 Downing Street was from the explosion of British artillery shells. On 11 September 1940, for instance, the very day that the anti-aircraft barrage began, there was a direct hit on Westminster Abbey, the first of the war. An anti-aircraft shell fell in Old Palace Yard, between the Abbey and the House of Lords, and exploded, blowing out several very old leaded windows. That same day, Parliament was struck for the first time, when an artillery shell landed on the Commons library. An hour later another shell caused several casualties when it landed on

Horse Guards Avenue. On 13 September, an anti-aircraft shell exploded on Horse Guards Parade, causing some damage to the windows and roof of No 10 Downing Street. On the same day, another shell landed near Westminster Abbey's West Door. Four days later, No 10 Downing Street was struck again by the shelling when a fragment of one anti-aircraft shell penetrated the air-raid shelter in the garden. It was becoming clear that there were disadvantages to giving the gun crews a free hand.

This book is mostly concerned with civilian casualties of friendly fire, but of course soldiers and police officers were also being killed by the artillery pounding London and other cities. One such person was a young soldier called William Sim.

William Munro Sim was born on 11 May 1915 in Sandhaven, a small fishing village in Scotland. At the age of 20 he signed up to join the army, serving for three years in the Scots Guards. After being discharged from the army, Sim joined the Southend police and from 20 February 1939 patrolled the streets as a constable. He was obviously well settled in Southend, because on 12 October that same year, he married Minnie Hayward. The newly-married couple moved into a house at 32 Seaforth Grove in Southend.

Just two weeks after William Sim's wedding, he was recalled to the colours and returned to his old regiment, the Scots Guards, and posted to the Tower of London. His wife was now pregnant and gave birth to a baby boy in August 1940. Sim was now a lance corporal and when the Blitz began in September, he was involved in supporting the emergency services. On 19 September, he was helping the Auxiliary Fire Service near St Paul's Cathedral. As he ran to assist somebody in Newgate Street, an anti-aircraft shell exploded nearby and a splinter passed through the young man's heart. He was just 25 years of age.

It is important to remember that although that the bombing began in London, it later affected many provincial cities. We will now turn to a couple of other tragedies, typical of many. One happened in the south of England two months after the bombing began and the other in the Midlands a month later.

The city of Portsmouth, on the south coast of England, was a natural target for the German air force, being a major naval base. It was bombed during the Battle of Britain and harassed intermittently from 11 July 1940. Four miles to the west of Portsmouth, near the town of Lee-on-Solent, was a Royal Navy aerodrome which had been used during the First World War as a seaplane training base. This was renamed HMS *Daedalus* in 1939 and a number of naval air squadrons were based there at various times. Some members of the Women's Royal Naval Service were also attached to HMS *Daedalus* during the war and these women, known universally as Wrens, were billeted in Lee-on-Solent, rather than living on the base.

Some of the Wrens from HMS *Daedalus* were staying at the Mansfield House Hotel, which had been requisitioned by the War Office. On the evening of Saturday, 23 November 1940, twenty-four of them sat down in the dining room and prepared to eat. An air raid was taking place at the time – bombs were falling and the anti-aircraft guns were firing back at the bombers. We remark on something now which we shall later being looking at in detail, the surprising fact that many people simply didn't take cover during air raids, either in a shelter or elsewhere. Even in London, at the height of the Blitz, only a minority of people sheltered during a raid. Around 60 per cent either stayed in their homes or went about their business as usual. Almost as soon as the young women had taken their seats, an artillery shell smashed through the window and then exploded above the table around which they were seated. Of those present, ten died almost immediately. The youngest of these were three 19-year-olds: Joyce Millicent Bennett, Winnie Blackett and Beryl Melita Northfield. Most of the others who were killed were in their twenties. Apart from the dead, thirteen of the women were injured, some of them very gravely. Only one of those present that evening escaped without any injury at all.

There were a number of anti-aircraft batteries around Lee-on-Solent and it was impossible to say from which of them the fatal shell had come. A couple of miles away at Stokes Bay were some 4.5in naval guns which had been in action that night and there were other heavy guns at Portsmouth. In 1996 a commemorative plaque was fixed to the wall of the building which had once been the Mansfield House Hotel.

Just in case it should be thought that the death of the ten Wrens at Lee-on-Solent was a freak event, we turn to the Midlands, at that time the industrial heartland of England, for something which happened the month following the tragedy in Lee-on-Solent. Tipton is a municipal borough which lies between Birmingham and Wolverhampton. During the

Second World War, the West Midlands was heavily bombed, the city of Coventry coming to symbolize for many the destruction of the Blitz. Tipton is in the middle of this area and suffered a number of casualties. What is not generally known is that more people were killed in Tipton by British artillery than died through the German bombing. One especially terrible instance will serve to show why this might have been.

On the evening of Saturday, 21 December 1940, everything was peaceful in the Midlands. Although there would be a bombing raid the following night, nothing was happening that day. Anti-aircraft guns were positioned on Rowley Hills, near Tipton. These were manned by the 40th Worcestershire (Rowley Regis) Battalion of the Home Guard, who were that day practising the drill of loading their guns and setting the time on the fuzes. In the nearby hamlet of Tividale, a wedding reception was being held at the Boat Inn. Sidney Jones and Florence Pottinger had been married that afternoon and now a modest party was being held to celebrate the event. Some of the party were in the bar, which was warmed by a cast iron stove, while others stood outside smoking. Several children were present.

The Home Guard detachment on Rowley Hills had cleaned one of their guns and somebody had the idea of loading a shell in the breech, so that it would be ready to fire at once the next time that there was an air raid. Having done so, a second man promptly came along and adjusted the elevation of the gun and, not realizing that it was loaded, pressed the firing lever. The 28lb shell then flew into the air and, returning to earth almost vertically, fell straight down the chimney of the Boat Inn at Tividale. Once it reached the cast iron stove at the foot of the chimney, it exploded with devastating force, killing twelve people outright and maiming many others. Among the dead were the bride and her young brother. Sidney Jones, the groom, was not killed, but both his legs were blown off in the explosion.

The two examples of multiple deaths from artillery fire above are by no means unusual. It was certainly more common for one or two people to die at a time, rather than a dozen or so, as at Lee-on-Solent and Tividale, but then of course that was the case too with German bombs. Returning to London, we see that Police Constable Thomas McHattie, aged 44, was killed by an anti-aircraft shell on 17 October 1940 and that PC Harold Lambert died in the same way on 9 December that year.

The artillery barrage launched by the British army before the battle of the Somme in 1916 has become a byword for operations of that type during the First World War. In the week before the British troops went 'over the top', the artillery pounded the German lines relentlessly, firing a total of 1,738,000 shells onto the enemy positions. By comparison, the British barrage over and on London went on night after night, with only a night or two's break in November, from 11 September 1940 to 11 May 1941. The number of shells fired each night was almost incredible. On the night of 14 October 1940, a total of 8,326 shells were fired in and around London. On other nights, over 13,000 shells were fired. Of course, the number varied from night to night, but when you consider that the artillery was firing for 240 nights or so, the total number of shells certainly exceeded that used in the run-up to the Somme! Remember, these were not being fired at German trenches, but in and above the streets of London.

Readers are invited to consider how many casualties might be expected as a result of this massive bombardment, which was greatest in the capital but included all the major cities of Britain. This then is part of the secret blitz, a military assault on urban population centres by troops who were supposedly guarding them and protecting civilians from harm.

Some readers will perhaps be asking themselves why so many of the artillery shells fired at the German aeroplanes should instead have failed to explode until they landed in the cities which they were supposed to be protecting. There are three reasons, two of them closely linked. The first lies in the mechanical process of setting off the shells, when once they had been fired. Without going into too much tedious mechanical detail, the shells fired by the anti-aircraft guns of the Second World War used in the main clockwork timing devices. Some were detonated by the change in barometric pressure as they soared thousands of feet into the air, but most were triggered by devices very much like modern-day kitchen timers, the sort of thing which can be set to sound an alarm after five, ten or thirty minutes. In the case of the AA shells, the times were in seconds, rather than minutes. These fuzes would be set before the shell was loaded and fired. The action of being propelled into the air would cause the timer to start running and it would then trigger the detonation of the shell a certain number of seconds after it had been fired. So, for example, if it was thought that the aeroplanes were flying at 24,000ft and the shell would take 12 seconds to climb to that height, then the fuze would be set for 12 seconds.

Now, manufacturing delicate pieces of clockwork which are capable of surviving and working correctly despite the enormous acceleration to which an artillery shell is subjected, requires a great deal of skill. Before the start of the Second World War, most of the time-delay fuzes used in British artillery shells were purchased from the German company Thiel. Another German firm called Junghans and a Swiss company, Dixi, also manufactured such fuzes. Needless to say, after September 1939, the supply of such devices was abruptly cut off and Britain was forced to make their own. The Germans and Swiss, of course, had a long tradition of watchmaking and the clockwork mechanisms they produced were superb. It did not prove possible to develop from scratch similarly fine craftsmanship in British-made timers. In fact, one scientist who was in the early years of the war working on an invention which would supersede the clockwork fuze, the proximity fuze, claimed bluntly that more than half of the fuzes produced by the British failed to work properly and as a result that half the anti-aircraft shells fired only exploded when they returned to earth.

In the final chapter of this book, we shall be looking at the development by Britain and the United States of the proximity fuze, designed to detonate shells when their target was in range, rather than at some predetermined time. Jack Allen, one of the scientists working at Cambridge University's Cavendish Laboratory, was in a very good position to know about the shortcomings of the time fuzes currently in use. His views on the subject were not off-the-cuff remarks, but the considered opinion of a man who was working hard upon a development that many people thought to be as important as the atomic bomb project in America. Allen said that fully half the fuzes on the shells being manufactured in Britain after 1939 were defective. He suggested that this meant that half the AA shells being fired into the sky above Britain's cities failed to explode when they should and fell to earth, only detonating when they landed. It was his belief that at least as many Londoners were being killed during the Blitz by shells as were dying as a result of German bombs.

A quick calculation will show the implication of what Jack Allen was saying, if he were correct. The Blitz did not of course affect only London. Provincial cities such as Manchester, Coventry and Liverpool were also targeted by the Luftwaffe. The 'Christmas Blitz' on Manchester took place on the nights of 22 and 23 December 1940. On the first night, German bombers dropped 272 tons of high explosives on the city, along with thousands of incendiaries. The following night, they returned, this time delivering 195 tons of high explosive bombs and again, many incendiaries. Hundreds of people died during these two air raids – 363 in Manchester and 197 in nearby Salford. It is when we look at what was being done to defend the city that a problem emerges.

Because Manchester was a manufacturing centre, with many factories producing parts for aircraft and tanks, it had been expected that sooner or later attempts would be made to hit the city's industrial sites. Anti-aircraft guns had accordingly been set up on many open spaces in the city, for example parks and large gardens. On the two nights of the Christmas Blitz, these AA guns fired a total of 29,000 shells above Manchester. Most of the guns would have been 3.7in ones, firing shells weighing 28lbs. Some guns would have been much larger and a few smaller, so it is reasonable to take the average weight of these shells as being around 30lbs. This leads to the astonishing conclusion that at the same time that the Germans were dropping 467 tons of bombs on Manchester, the British were firing 388 tons of artillery shells.

It is impossible to know precisely how many of the shells fired over the two nights of the Christmas Blitz were defective. Suppose, just for argument's sake, that we accept the suggestion made by the scientist working on the proximity fuze, that half the British AA shells exploded only when they struck the ground. This would mean that something in the region of 194 tons of shells would be exploding on the streets of Manchester, alongside the 467 tons of bombs. This is bad enough, almost a third of the explosive power devastating Manchester those nights being provided by British artillery, but there is worse. Look again Illustration 3, which shows the nosecone of an AA shell. It weighs about a pound. Imagine 14,500 of these falling onto Manchester and landing at 200 miles per hour. Now picture another 194 tons of assorted scrap iron, also hitting the streets at a similar speed. And all to what end? Just two bombers were brought down by those 29,000 shells, one crashing onto Trafford Park and the other coming down in the sea near Blackpool.

Common sense tells us that if the figures about defective fuzes are correct then, around a third of the casualties in Manchester over the two nights at which we have just been looking are likely to have been killed by the British defences, rather than the German attackers. One simply cannot hurl almost 400 tons of high-explosive shells over and at a city without expecting heavy casualties. This is not the whole story though. Both in Manchester and throughout the rest of Britain, other factors were at play.

That many of the shells being produced for and fired by British anti-aircraft artillery were defective would, in itself, be enough by itself to account for a lot of the incidents of friendly-fire casualties in Britain during the Second World War. Two more factors things must be considered though. Setting the fuzes was itself a fiddly matter requiring patience and attention to detail. When one is working in pitch darkness, due to the blackout, and bombs are exploding nearby, it would not be in the least surprising if errors were to be made. This is in the nature of battlefield conditions. After some engagements in the American Civil War, it was found that many soldiers had reloaded their muskets by ramming wadding, powder and balls down the barrels of their muzzle-loading weapons six or seven times. They had however forgotten the minor detail of actually firing their guns and so the barrels were full to the brim with successive, unfired charges! This is the sort of thing which can happen in the heat of battle.

What frequently happened, and not only in Britain, was that shells would be fired without anybody adjusting the timer on the fuze. These would then fly up into the air, sail past the enemy aeroplanes and then return to earth, where they would explode on impact with the ground. Mishaps like this were common with even the best trained of soldiers. Of course, an awful lot of the men operating Britain's anti-aircraft guns were not the best-trained men in the army at all. Men, in other words, whom no other unit wanted. Once all the other army, navy and air force units had had their pick, those who were left were often assigned to the anti-aircraft guns. The standard of such troops really was abysmal. Writing in a special supplement to the *London Gazette*, published on 18 December 1947, General Pile did not pull any punches when referring to the quality of the troops who ended up manning the anti-aircraft guns:

> It very soon became evident that the quality of the conscripts allotted to the Command was inferior and that I was not

> receiving such a good selection of the Army intake as other arms. This was due to restrictions as to age and medical fitness on the men to be posted to Arms liable to serve overseas, and I later had occasion to protest against a process of allocation of manpower which involved the posting of the best type of recruits to other Arms at the expense of A.A. Command.

In a book which he wrote, called *Ack Ack*, Pile gave specific examples of what he meant by the anti-aircraft batteries not getting 'the best type of recruits':

> Many were quite unsuited for military duty, let alone the highly technical duties of AA. Out of 25 who arrived at a fairly representative battery, one had a withered arm, one was mentally deficient, one had a glass eye which fell out whenever he doubled to the guns, and two were in the advanced and more obvious stages of venereal disease.

When we consider the above circumstances in combination, the surprise is not that so many shells exploded at the wrong time, but rather that any actually went off near the aeroplanes that they were meant to destroy. These inadequate troops were expected to carry out the most intricate calculations relating to the height speed and bearing of approaching aircraft whilst under fire and usually in the dark. They then had to work out how long to set the fuzes for and set them correctly. Even if all this was accomplished successfully, there still remained a reported 50/50 chance that the fuze would in any case be defective and fail to operate as required.

We saw how a dozen people from a wedding party were inadvertently killed by faulty procedures at one AA battery, let us now look at another case of the same type, a little later in the war. The district of Lanishen, in the north of the Welsh city of Cardiff, is famous today for its tax offices, which are housed in the tallest building for miles around. In 1944 though, Lanishen was better known as the location of a 50-acre complex of factories, known as Cardiff Royal Ordnance Factories. These produced field guns for the British army. Because of its industry and importance to the war effort, the Luftwaffe bombed Cardiff pretty regularly between

1940 and 1943, killing a total of 387 people in the course of the Second World War. The last German bombing raid took place on18 May 1943.

The Cardiff Royal Ordnance Factories were naturally a target for German attacks, but they still stood, relatively unscathed, as the war entered its penultimate year in 1944. By the end of March that year, the dropping of bombs from aeroplanes flying over Britain had all but ceased and the stage was set for the arrival of the V weapons, the cruise missile known as the 'doodlebug' and the ballistic missile called the V 2. There was, however, some slight activity over South Wales by German bombers on the night of Monday, 27 March 1944. That night, many women were working at lathes and other power tools in the factory in Lanishen.

There had been an air-raid warning on the evening of 27 March, but because no bombs had been dropped on Cardiff for almost a year, the workers in the factory did not head for an air-raid shelter but simply stayed at their machines. Up on the high ground around Cardiff, a number of 3.7in anti-aircraft guns were positioned and these fired at aeroplanes which were seen over the Bristol Channel. One gun, at St Athan Road, Gabalfa, for reasons which were never explained, fired a shell in the opposite direction to the aeroplanes, sending it over north Cardiff. We see here a perfect example of how the factors at which we looked above could combine in lethal ways. On the one hand is the fact that a piece of artillery was pointed in the wrong direction, probably human error by a gun crew. This in itself would not have been a disaster, except that it is very likely that the shell fired had a faulty fuze, which caused it to explode when it returned to earth, rather than at 20,000ft in the air. As it was, the artillery shell which had been fired in the direction of north Cardiff soared into the sky, failed to explode at the correct altitude and then fell like a stone towards Lanishen. By ill fortune, it landed on the roof of the Royal Ordnance Factory.

The factory at Lanishen was divided up into various 'shops', machine shops which were indicated by letters of the alphabet. The 28lb shell crashed through the glass roof of Machine Shop P, the glass not being strong enough to trigger the fuze. It then struck a metal junction box, high up in the roof-space, which caused it to detonate. Razor-sharp fragments of red-hot metal were sprayed down onto the men and women below. Most of those working in P Shop were women, including 20-year-old Miss W. Bishton. Her 47-year-old father, who was working in A Shop, had come

1. A twin QF 5.25in turret on board HMS *King George V*.

2. Similar guns set up on the top of London's Primrose Hill.

3. The nosecone of a 3.7in shell which fell on London in 1940.

4. A 3.7in anti-aircraft gun at Mudchute, on the Isle of Dogs.

5. The world's first anti-aircraft gun, used in 1871; the German *Ballonabwehrkanone*.

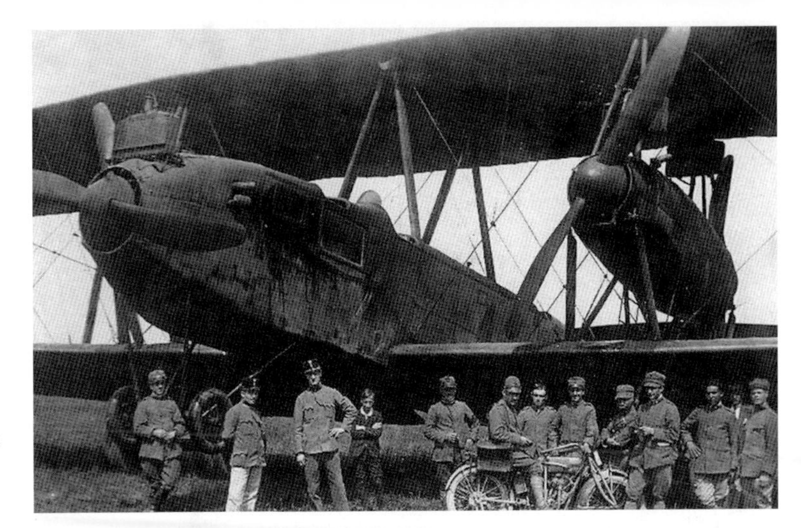

6. A German Gotha, the aeroplane used to bomb London in 1917–18.

7. Bomb damage caused in 1915 to a sphinx at the base of Cleopatra's Needle.

8. QF 1-pounder Mk II 37mm 'pom-pom' gun, used in the First World War as an anti-aircraft gun.

(*Above*) 9. A 3in naval gun at Tilbury Fort in Essex, the standard anti-aircraft gun of the First World War.

(*Left*) 10. A house in South London which was destroyed by a German bomb during the First World War.

11. 'Consol' shelter or 'firewatcher's bell' from the Second World War.

12. A 4.5in naval gun on Clapham Common.

13. Another naval gun on Wanstead Flats in East London.

(*Above*) 14. A Second World War 3.7in anti-aircraft gun at Tilbury Fort in Essex.

(*Left*) 15. A pair of 40mm Bofors guns aboard HMS *Belfast*.

(*Above*) 16. Brompton Road tube station, the former HQ of the AA forces in London.

(*Below*) 17. Le Havre after bombing by the British and Americans. (La Havre Municipal Archives)

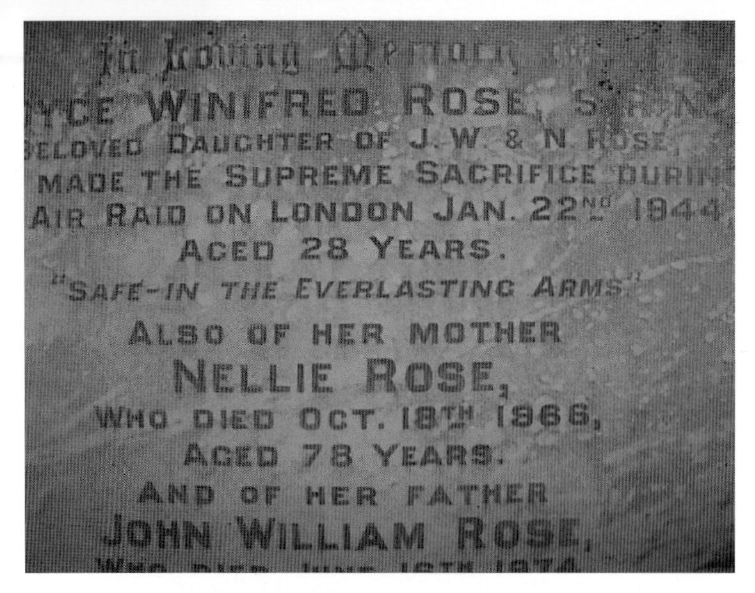

ACED 28 YEARS.
"SAFE-IN THE EVERLASTING ARMS."
ALSO OF HER MOTHER
NELLIE ROSE,
WHO DIED OCT. 18TH 1966,
ACED 78 YEARS.
AND OF HER FATHER
JOHN WILLIAM ROSE,

18. Grave of a nurse from Shropshire who was a friendly-fire casualty in the Blitz.

19. Plaque at Bethnal Green tube station, commemorating the 'worst civilian disaster of the Second World War'.

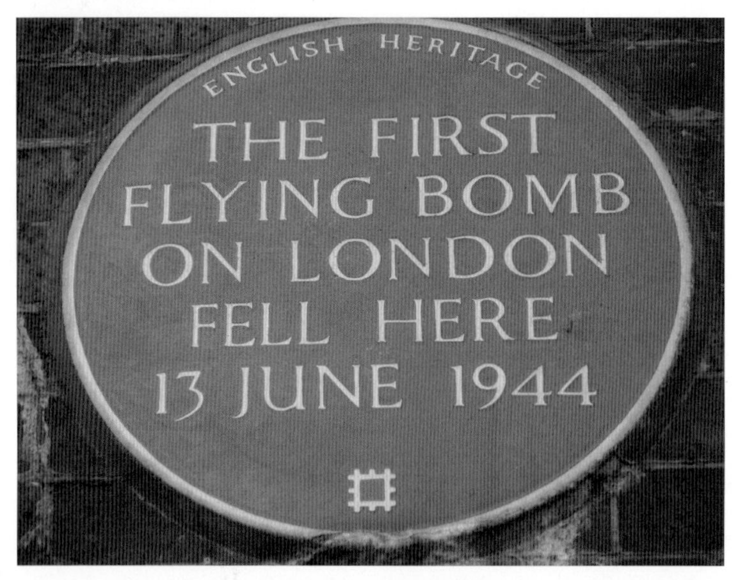

ENGLISH HERITAGE
THE FIRST
FLYING BOMB
ON LONDON
FELL HERE
13 JUNE 1944

20. Plaque at the railway bridge across Grove Road, marking the spot where the first V 1 landed in London.

to say hello to her before starting his own shift. Both were killed, along with ten other people. The local newspaper, the *Western Mail*, reported the incident on 29 March by stating that:

> Anti-aircraft shells, one of which exploded in a crowded factory, killing 12 people, including seven women, and injuring as many more, were the chief cause of damage during activity over the South Wales coastal area on Monday night.

The deaths at Lanishen illustrate a most significant point. We see that the journalist who wrote the piece in the *Western Mail* had little doubt about the reality of the situation created by the artillery fire that night: 'Anti-aircraft shells . . . were the chief cause of damage . . .' This was only obvious when the effects of the artillery fire was not masked by the explosion of a lot of bombs being dropped from aeroplanes. Hardly any bombs were dropped on that Monday night and so it was glaringly obvious what had caused the deaths, injuries and damage to property. This sheds light upon the way that the role of the British in the deaths of the Blitz has become hidden. In Chapter 2 we saw that during the bombing of Southend, on 26 May 1915, just three people died. One was killed by a German bomb and two by British artillery. It is often the case that when we are able to examine in minute detail the causes of the various casualties during the bombing of Britain in both the First and Second World Wars, we find that artillery and not bombs are the chief culprit. When deaths run into hundreds or thousands though, there is a natural tendency to dismiss them as being a consequence of 'enemy action'. The tragedy at Tipton in the Midlands shows how this worked with light casualties.

The Midlands in England were, because of the concentration of industry there, a popular target for the Luftwaffe during the Second World War. The destruction of Coventry is often cited as the worst instance of the attacks on the Midlands. The borough of Tipton, in the heart of this area, was also bombed and British artillery tried to shoot down the aeroplanes as they flew over. During the course of the war, 23 civilians were killed in Tipton during the air raids. Nine of these died when German bombs exploded near them and twelve were killed when an anti-aircraft shell landed on a public house during the celebration of a wedding. In other words, over half of the dead were killed by the British, rather than the Germans.

So far, we have been looking at the death of British civilians caused directly by the artillery of their own side, but there is another way that the anti-aircraft guns were responsible for killing the people whom they were supposedly protecting. Much mention was made in the newspapers of the time of the fact that at times exploding anti-aircraft shells were so conspicuous in the sky that it caused German planes to turn back. This is represented to readers as a triumph of defence. A few moments thought will soon show that the consequences of such an action were devastating for Londoners.

It was all very well for scientists sitting in their laboratories to calculate that the odds of any aeroplane being shot out of the sky by an anti-aircraft shell were virtually zero, but for any pilots heading towards London while thousands of shells were exploding in the air ahead of them, matters might have presented themselves rather differently. Some bombers did indeed, as newspapers reported, 'turn back' from the barrage, but this did not mean that civilians were not killed by their bombs. The crew of such planes would not wish to return to their airfields with a full load of bombs, partly because of the dangers of landing with a few tons of bombs on board, but also because they would then have faced accusations of cowardice from their superior officers. The solution to this dilemma was simple. They dropped their bombs on the eastern suburbs of London before turning for home. This might have prevented harm to the strategic targets in and around London towards they had been heading, but ensured that the streets of districts such as Ilford and West Ham would be blown to pieces instead.

We have in this chapter looked at some of the direct effects of artillery fire on British targets, that is to say heavy shells exploding in factories, hotels and public houses. Such incidents were, in the main, caused by shells not behaving as they were intended to do, due to defective fuzes or fuzes which had not been correctly set. In the next chapter we shall be thinking about the consequence for civilians when the shells did as they were supposed to do and exploded thousands of feet in the air. Before doing so, we need to remind ourselves what we have so far learned.

We know of course by now that the chances of any shell destroying an enemy bomber were negligible and that they posed far more of a hazard to civilians on the ground than they did to German bomber crews. But the way that they were used, combined with other actions taken to protect against bombers, practically guaranteed that the civilian death toll would be inflated. Firing heavy barrages of shells meant in the first instance that bombers would fly as high as possible in order to avoid the exploding shells. This move meant that there was not the remotest possibility of their bombs being dropped accurately on any target. When bombing the London docks, it was inevitable that because of the height at which the bombs were released that many of them would miss the docks themselves and land in nearby streets.

The great height at which the bombs were released made accuracy improbable, but the blackout made it impossible. The best that could be hoped for was that the bombers would fly over some specific area and drop bombs on it. Often, even this was not achieved, because of the fierceness of the anti-aircraft fire. The bombs would simply be dropped anywhere and the plane would then return to its base. The blackout and anti-aircraft fire therefore combined to massively increase the civilian deaths near the original targets, for example the docks or factories which the bombers had in mind to strike. Most people seemed simply to take all this for granted. They liked to hear the sound of the artillery and even though they knew that it was not very effective, it was still a comforting thought that the Germans were not having it all their own way.

Some readers might think that the casualties from British artillery that are the subject of this book are only now being revealed because perhaps censorship during the war prevented anybody from knowing about them, but this is a quite mistaken view. The injury, destruction and death caused by AA fire was not only common knowledge, it was widely reported in the newspapers at the time. On Saturday, 15 February 1941, in the middle of the Blitz, the *Belfast Telegraph* had a headline above a column of its front page, which read, 'SIX PEOPLE KILLED WHEN BOMB FELL NEAR LONDON CHURCH'. Beneath this is a smaller headline, which says, 'DAMAGE AA SHELLS CAUSED'. There is a brief account of the bomb which fell near a church and killed six people, including a soldier. The article continues:

> What was at first thought to be bombs dropped from enemy raiders at one point in London turned out to be two of our A.A.

> shells which exploded on striking the ground. One man was killed and a woman was seriously injured. They were passing along the street at the time.

There is no change of pace in the piece, as it moves from deaths from a German bomb to a death caused by a British shell. There follows a description of various other people killed by bombing and then at the end there is this:

> During heavy gunfire in Romford and Hornchurch, Essex, an A.A. shell struck a concrete shelter in the rear garden of a house and exploded. The occupants of the shelter, Mr and Mrs Bishop, both about 45 years of age, were severely injured and taken to hospital. They have since died.

The fact is that British newspapers were reporting injuries and deaths resulting from anti-aircraft fire almost from the beginning of the Blitz. It was certainly no secret to anybody at the time that AA guns were inflicting casualties on their own side. Newspapers reported only especially awful cases of this happening, because they knew as well as their readers that it was a common-enough occurrence and scarcely worth mentioning unless there was some remarkable circumstance associated with it.

It is only since the end of the Second World War that people have tended to keep quiet about the death toll from British artillery, perhaps because as the myth of the Battle of Britain and Blitz have grown over the years, it seems a shame to spoil the story with too many facts.

We have looked in this chapter chiefly at shells which did not behave as they should have done, that is to say those which exploded on the ground, rather than in the air. In the next chapter we are going to look at the dangerous effects of artillery shells which *did* behave as expected, that is to say those which exploded tens of thousands of feet above the ground. The accounts of those who were present in cities during the air raids by the Luftwaffe suggest that the shells which were not faulty or mishandled caused at least as many civilian deaths as those which malfunctioned.

Chapter 6

Hiding in Plain Sight: The Menace of Shrapnel, 1940–1944

Readers might, despite the mass of evidence so far adduced, still be feeling a little dubious about the whole idea of anti-aircraft fire killing civilians in the way which has been outlined. Perhaps they are asking themselves why they have never heard of these massacres and how such shocking events could possibly have become hidden from view. The truth is that they never have been hidden: they have been there all along, staring us in the face. It is simply that our own preconceptions have blinded us to what happened in Britain between 1940 and 1944. One or two instances of how our perception causes us to miss what is right in front of us might be helpful.

Illustration 11 is of a stout metal sentry box, commonly seen in Britain during the Second World War. This one is from the Museum of London's Dockland site on the Isle of Dogs. There is another of these things, which are known as Consol shelters, in London's Imperial War Museum. In the autumn of 2018 a party of schoolchildren were being led around this museum by their teachers. The Consol shelter in the War Museum is simply labelled as an 'air-raid shelter' and these children, who were obviously studying the Second World War at school, were fascinated by it, asking many questions of the adults who were accompanying them, questions such as, 'How would it protect you from a bomb?' and 'What's the use of a shelter which isn't underground?' They had a point and one is reminded of the old saying about truth coming from 'Out of the mouths of babes and sucklings'. These children, none of whom were above the age of 11, had struck upon a very interesting point, one which had probably occurred to few adults.

We know that above-ground air-raid shelters were around during the Blitz, although very few people wished to use them, partly because they were crowded and insanitary, but chiefly due to their vulnerability to bomb-blasts. A structure like a glorified garden shed, built only of bricks and mortar, provides little protection from a bomb-blast. They were colloquially known as 'Morrison Sandwiches', named after Home Secretary Herbert Morrison. When a blast caused the walls to collapse, the thick concrete roof fell onto the shelterers, crating the 'sandwich'. We all know that to shelter safely from air raids, one went underground, either to a Tube station or into an Anderson shelter in the back garden.

What use would the giant tin seen in Illustration 11 have been as an air-raid shelter? Granted, it was made of bulletproof steel, but even so, it would provide little or no protection from a bomb exploding nearby. These shelters, produced in Birmingham, were commonly known as 'firewatchers' bells'. This meant that the door was usually left open, so that the firewatcher could actually watch for fires, which would have reduced their effectiveness as a shelter from bombs to almost zero.

Let us look at another curious point, of which most people are aware but the significance of which eludes almost everybody. In the well-known television comedy *Dad's Army*, Bill Pertwee plays the instantly recognizable character of ARP Warden Hodges. His catchphrase of, 'Put that light out!' is as familiar to us as the steel helmet which he wears, which has a large 'W' painted on the front of it. So used are we to seeing images from the Second World War of ARP wardens and police officers wearing these broad-brimmed helmets, that we seldom stop to ask ourselves exactly what they were meant to shield their wearers from. Just as with the Consol shelter, it can hardly have been exploding bombs!

Here is a question which may, on the face of it, sound utterly absurd, 'What is the main danger during an air raid by enemy bombers?' The answer must surely be that the danger lies in being injured or killed by explosions. In Britain, during the Second World War, this was not the case. Scientific advisors to the Prime Minister carried out experiments with monkeys and other animals, exposing them to the effects of blast, and found that death from this cause was not common. What almost invariably killed the animals and also people caught in air raids was not the explosion of the bomb, but being buried in the aftermath or having a piece of shrapnel or debris driven into their body. It was the speed of such material and the site of its entry which determined whether or not it would cause serious injury or death. A small, fast-moving piece of metal striking the head would be far more likely to kill than a larger piece of debris hitting the leg at a slower speed.

In the last chapter we looked at the deaths and destruction of property caused by heavy artillery shells which had defective fuzes or whose fuzes had been improperly set. This was a serious problem. Although we have touched upon it though, we have not really examined in any detail the effect of the rain of shrapnel which resulted from the shells which exploded as they were supposed to, that is to say, thousands of feet in the air.

To begin with, we remind ourselves of the official advice of the British government, a few months before the start of the Second World War. *Air Raid Warnings*, published at the beginning of 1939, says that 'most of the injuries in an air raid are caused not by direct hits by bombs but by flying fragments of debris or by bits of shells'. This immediately explains the significance of both Warden Hodges' helmet and also the peculiar little steel air-raid shelter in Illustration 11. They are neither of them designed to stop people being injured by explosions on the ground, but rather they protect from objects falling from above. Bombardier Bill Church was part of the crew of a 3.7in anti-aircraft gun near Wormwood Scrubs Prison. It was the same type of artillery as that shown in Illustrations 4 and 14. In later years, he mentioned the importance of tin helmets, writing:

> Casualties from German bombs were light. The most dangerous thing was shrapnel coming back down. You could sometimes hear it bouncing off your helmet, and there would also be quite a few duds coming down.

Now we see the real purpose of the helmets warn by AA gunners, air raid wardens and the police. They were to prevent head injuries from pieces of metal falling from very high up, metal produced not by German bombs, but by the anti-aircraft shells being fired by the British soldiers on the ground.

Before exploring this aspect of air raids further, we should perhaps stop and consider one or two things about bombs and artillery shells. Bombs and shells which explode on the ground waste a good deal of their power in gouging out craters. If the aim of your bomb, and this applies just as much to nuclear weapons as it does to the kind of high-explosive bombs being dropped by the German air force during the Blitz, is to kill as many people as possible, then you really want it to go off in the air, not after hitting the ground. The aim is for the full force of the blast to be directed downwards, on the people below, not used in digging out a pointless hole in the earth. This is why the atomic bomb dropped on Hiroshima was caused to explode above the city and not merely when it hit the ground.

There is quite an art in arranging for shells to explode before landing at their target, in order to maximise injuries. We shall be looking in the final chapter of this book at the development of the proximity fuze, which did so much to increase the effectiveness of anti-aircraft fire. Shells fitted with such fuzes needed no fiddly timing devices, which were so prone to human error. Instead, they contained a miniature radar transmitter which bounced radio signals around until they echoed from a nearby object, either the ground or an aeroplane. When these reflected signals were received, they triggered the shell to explode. This was useful not only when firing at, for example, V 1 flying bombs, but also if one wished to target a group of infantry and kill as many of them as possible.

Understanding the principle of air bursts, as opposed to ground bursts, enables us to see where a lot of the real danger came from during a Second World War air raid. A bomb or shell landing on the ground and exploding would not only use half its power to dig a crater, its actual explosive force through the air was also limited. Some people might be killed by the blast, but not all that many. Taken as an average in Britain over the whole course of the war, roughly 70,000 tons of explosives were dropped by the Germans and about 60,000 people killed. This works out at about one person killed for every ton of munitions which was detonated. The great majority of these explosions were of course ground bursts, the Germans not having been able to develop an effective proximity fuze.

Deaths from air bursts are in the main caused by bits of metal being driven downwards at great speed and striking down an enemy like a hail of bullets. It is against this danger that steel helmets of the type worn by Warden Hodges were first developed during the First World War. In 1914, British troops sent off to France wearing peaked caps made of ordinary cloth. It was soon discovered that this put them at enormous hazard from fragments of exploding shells and so the following year the so-called 'Brodie' helmet, designed by a man called John Brodie, was introduced. It is the 'Brodie' helmet which we see in pictures of civil defence in wartime Britain.

Of course, the shrapnel from the artillery shells fired up into the sky by the British was not driven into the bodies of its victims with explosive force, but was rather subject to the laws of nature, after having fallen from 15,000, 20,000 or 30,000ft. Such scrap iron was as deadly as that produced by a shell or bomb exploding nearer to the victim, as a few simple calculations will soon show us.

In recent years, television news broadcast have shown us the firing of what are sometimes known as 'joy bullets'. It is common practice in certain of the more lawless Middle Eastern countries to celebrate military victories, marriages, funerals or perhaps even the birth of a child, by firing an automatic rifle into the air. The bullets fired in this way travel up at a speed of 700 metres per second, until the force of gravity slows them to a halt. They then fall under their own weight back to the ground, accelerating under the pull of gravity until they reach their terminal velocity. A bullet falling from 3,000–4,000ft can gain quite sufficient momentum in this way to be travelling at a lethal speed by the time it reaches the ground.

There are many cases of deaths resulting from the practice of firing 'joy bullets' in Arab countries and there are also well-documented instances of it happening in the United States, where firearms are alarmingly common. A few seconds after midnight on the night of 31 December 2014, a man called Javier Suarez Rivera stood outside his home in Houston, celebrating the New Year with his family. They were outside the house, watching the fireworks which lit up the sky, when Rivera gave a cry and fell to the ground, blood gushing from a wound in the top of his skull. A bullet fired playfully into the air, as an accompaniment to the fireworks, had gone up and then fallen down again under the force of gravity, to penetrate the head of somebody over a mile away. Some Americans have acquired the habit of celebrating with 'joy bullets' in this way and the consequences can be deadly.

Bullets of course are small and light, compared with some of the shrapnel produced by an exploding artillery shell. We look again at Illustration 3 and imagine this piece of metal plummeting from a height of 30,000ft and landing on somebody's head. Almost certainly, an injury received in this way would be fatal. If we now imagine 10,000 heavy shells exploding high in the air one night and each one producing a shower of fragments, ranging in size from bullets to chunks weighing a kilogram, we begin to appreciate the nature of the problem.

One objection which might be raised is that most people would surely be safely in air-raid shelters during the night time, when the anti-aircraft guns were active. The shower of scrap metal might break a few roof-tiles or windows, but it would hardly be likely to injure people. They would mostly be under cover. Once again, we are deceived by the false image which has been propagated of the Blitz. Our vision is of people huddled on the platforms of Underground stations or in the Anderson shelter at the bottom of their gardens. An ounce or two of metal landing on the earth covering the Anderson shelter would do no harm, would it?

It may come as a surprise to learn that despite all the photographs which we see of people sheltering in the Tube, only about 4 per cent of Londoners used the Underground in this way during the Blitz. A few more, but still only 9 per cent, spent air raids in the unpopular public shelters and 27 per cent slept in Anderson shelters. These figures are taken from a survey conducted in London in November 1940. No fewer than 60 per cent of people living in London simply carried on with their lives, sleeping at home and walking the streets as usual. This seems almost beyond belief and yet it the case.

Just after the war, in late 1945, a book was published which was an attempt to tell, while memories were still fresh, the story of civil defence in Britain during the Second World War. *Citizens in War – And After* was written by Stephen Spender and contained a foreword by the wartime Home Secretary Herbert Morrison. Spender wrote of the first week of the Blitz:

> Londoners living in the West End tended rather to ignore the raids. Crowds walked home in the streets through bombing, and later through gunfire, and the restaurants stayed open until midnight. Walking home from the cinema or theatre or restaurant, people stamped out incendiaries in Piccadilly and at the edge of the park.

Later, after conceding that once the bombing became more widespread, theatres and restaurants began to close earlier than before the Blitz, Spender wrote:

> Yet people who read about the horrors of the Blitz after the war will probably fail to realize the extent to which life remained normal, with theatres open every evening, gentlemen dining at their clubs, and people walking to the office in the morning, with street cleaners gathering up the broken glass and piling it up along the sidewalk, as in the winter they do with the ice and snow.

The film *Gone With The Wind* had its UK premiere in London's Leicester Square in April 1940. It was still showing at a nearby cinema over four years later. At the height of the Blitz, with bombs falling across the West End, people were queuing in the streets to see the film.

It may seem strange to us to imagine that most people in London didn't bother with air-raid shelters and still popped into the West End to visit the cinemas and theatres, even with the Blitz in full swing, but there it is. These people were all well aware of the dangers entailed, the worst of which was believed to be not the bombs, but the constant barrage of metal falling from the heavens and liable to kill anybody whom it struck.

One final account of how the majority of people in British cities went out and about during the Blitz in more or less the same way that they had done in peacetime. Here is a reminiscence from a man who was 16 years old during the London Blitz. Peter Richards used to visit the cinema, go to a youth club and even run through the streets for exercise during air raids. He sometimes sheltered in a shop doorway if he heard anti-aircraft fire, because he knew that a rain of hot fragments of metal would soon be falling from the sky. Other than that, it was just a normal, teenage life:

> I used to go out running in the middle of the bombing. It's not that I didn't worry, but we took a calculated risk. We ran from the youth club in Bloomsbury to Regent's Park or ran round Bedford Square.

It is odd that this rain of hot, jagged pieces of metal falling on cities in vast quantities and at tremendous speeds has vanished from our collective memory. Those who lived through the Blitz frequently remark upon it as being so obvious a commonplace hazard as to be scarcely worth mentioning. Here is historian Correlli Barnett, writing in the *Independent* newspaper a few years ago. A teenager at the time of the Blitz, he mentions something which we have already touched upon, that life went on pretty much as usual and that people went out to cinemas and theatres just as before the war:

> Except during an air raid itself, the trains, trams and buses still ran; the theatres and cinemas stayed open. The cafés and restaurants did good business, even if the customers had to duck under the tables from time to time.

He continues:

> For others, the Blitz served as a liberating experience, as in the case of the spinster lady in our road who became an ambulance driver, undaunted by the crash of bombs and the clatter of falling shrapnel from burst anti-aircraft shells: a lady well able to cope with the dead or maimed bodies pulled from the rubble of a collapsed house.

The falling shrapnel is referred to in such a casual and matter-of-fact way that one wonders why such a mortal danger to life and limb should have become largely forgotten.

Not only was the shrapnel from anti-aircraft shells travelling at a great velocity by the time it reached the ground, it had two other characteristics which increased its ability to cause harm. It was, in the first place, jagged and with sharp edges. A bullet will usually pass into, and sometimes right through, the human body neatly, leaving a little hole with a diameter less than that of an ordinary pencil. This is not at all the case with a razor-sharp piece of twisted metal, which can slice open an arm or leg, severing arteries and veins in the process. The shrapnel was also very often white-hot when it landed, making it even more dangerous if it struck somebody on the way down. Here is Ron Mitchell, who was in the Home Guard during the Blitz:

> RAF involvement was mainly the contribution of light fighter/bombers and fighters equipped with the new airborne interception radar to intercept the German bomber formation at night and was not very effective at the time. Neither were the British anti-aircraft guns – numerous as they were. In fact, walking around London at night as I sometimes did with my friends, when not on Home Guard duty, was as dangerous from falling shrapnel (pieces of the anti-aircraft shells) as it was from bomb blast! For years after the war I kept two such pieces, quite large enough to at least injure. Both pieces were about one quarter inch thick, one was three inches in length, the other just over four – that had fallen close enough to me for me to find – after they had cooled off enough for me to pick up – not knowing how hot they would be I got badly blistered fingers the first time I attempted to pick one up! Frequently, when so walking, I would kick against or tread on such pieces – but, even more frequently there was the broken glass – everywhere, from the thin stuff of ordinary house windows to the thick plate glass of shop and store windows.

There are several points to note in this account. First, of course, is the fact that during air raids, this young man was simply strolling around without thinking of taking shelter. One of the reasons that anti-aircraft fire caused so many casualties is that plenty of people were out-of-doors and vulnerable to its effects. There is too the fact that the shrapnel was hot enough when he picked it up to blister his hands. The most important point of all though is that throwaway line in which this eyewitness to the Blitz mentions in passing that being out and about was 'as dangerous from falling shrapnel . . . as it was from bomb blast'.

Time and again in the reminiscences of those who lived through the Blitz, we find similar statements. These are not made with any emphasis, as though a startling revelation is being made. Rather, the fact that the British artillery fire was at least as dangerous as the German bombs is slipped in as an afterthought, something of which, it is assumed, everybody will be aware. It is the very strange to come across such references, equating the danger from the artillery with that from the bombs. It is probably fair to say that this is not something which has ever occurred to the average person, even those with an interest in the history of the Second World War.

In 2008, Gabriel Moshenska published a piece in the *Journal of Material Culture.* Entitled 'A Hard Rain: Children's Shrapnel Collections in the Second World War', the article included many interviews with people who were children in Britain during the Second World War. Here is part of one such interview:

> When the sirens used to go we went into the shelters, and when it was all clear we used to come out looking for shrapnel come down in the streets still hot. You picked it up in your hands and it was still hot, where it was come from the guns . . . you used to have the ack-ack guns driving round in the streets . . . they couldn't do much, I suppose it was more for morale. You see they were shooting at the planes, and when those shells explode the shrapnel's got to come down hasn't it.

This confirms in passing much of what we have already been looking at in this book, for example the idea of firing anti-aircraft guns purely to enhance civilian morale. Another of the interviewees revealed how widespread the falling shrapnel was, by saying:

> You could hear it come down on the roof, and you would hear a sort of tinkling sound in the evening when you were listening to the radio.

Moshenska goes on to say that:

> Tales of injuries and near misses from falling shrapnel are remarkably common in the sample, including head wounds where shrapnel hit or pierced steel helmets

The accounts in 'A Hard Rain' dovetail perfectly with the other first-hand stories at which we have so far looked, in that shrapnel from anti-aircraft shells which exploded thousands of feet overhead is shown to be both very common and also extremely dangerous, especially if one was standing or walking about in the open during an air raid. As Moshenshka says:

> With friends, neighbours, parents and teachers being killed and injured by falling shrapnel there is no doubt that many children were well aware of its very real dangers.

There was uneasiness at the time about the number of people being killed by artillery fire, as an exchange in the House of Commons in 1943 indicates. In March that year, a Member of Parliament rose to ask the Home Secretary a question. Independent MP Edgar Granville wanted to know:

> the number of civilian casualties in the London area from anti-aircraft shells and splinters during the enemy raid on London on 3rd March; and whether he will give a public warning of the dangers involved in standing in the open to watch the barrage during intensive anti-aircraft fire?

Home Secretary Herbert Morrison was too wily to be drawn into revealing exactly how many people were actually being killed by falling shrapnel and shells which exploded in the streets. He admitted that there had been such casualties but limited himself to saying:

> In districts in which bombs and anti-aircraft ammunition are falling together it is not always possible accurately to attribute casualties to the one cause or the other, but it is known that on the occasion in question some of the casualties were due solely to the latter cause. While in the circumstances it is not desirable to give detailed figures, I cannot too strongly emphasise that the public, unless their duties otherwise require, should not neglect the warnings so often given not to remain unnecessarily in an exposed position during an air raid, but should take cover in the nearest accessible shelter, including surface shelter.

In other words, people were certainly being killed by their own artillery fire, but the government did not want to say how many!

We made a few rough calculations in an earlier chapter to try and work out how many artillery shells might have exploded on the ground, rather than in the air. Let us now try and do the same thing for shell fragments falling from a great height. In London, anti-aircraft guns were firing perhaps 10,000 shells in a night. Taking as an average a weight of 30lbs and assuming that about a quarter of that weight would be taken up by the explosive charge within the shell, means that each shell would deposit somewhere in the region of 22.5lbs of steel fragments on the ground below. If, as we did before, we guess that 10 per cent of the shells did not explode in mid-air, then that would give us something over 9,000 which did. If we multiply 22.5 by 9,000, we find that 202,500lbs of metal would fall onto the streets of London in one night. This equates in metric terms to 91,852kg or over 90 metric tonnes of pieces of metal, every single night for months on end.

Some of the bits of metal would be little more than splinters or specks, but there would be many larger pieces, ranging in size from a bullet to the nosecone shown in Illustration 3. Because the nosecones of the shells invariably detached when they exploded, there could be around 9,000 of these crashing to the ground each night during the Blitz. That they could be deadly is seen when we look at newspaper reports from the time. The *Evening Despatch* for Tuesday, 17 December 1940, at the height of the Blitz, tells the story of 73-year-old Miss Hannah Maria Moore, who was living on the top floor of 89a Lea Street in Kidderminster. She went to bed during an air raid and the nosecone of a 3.7in shell fell from about 20,000ft, smashed through the roof of the house, penetrated the ceiling of the room in which Miss Moore was sleeping and struck her on the head, killing her instantly. The reminiscences of people who lived through the Blitz are full of stories of nearly being hit by big chunks of metal from anti-aircraft fire. Such anecdotes come of course from the survivors. Here are four more stories from people who provided personal accounts to the BBC's archive about the Second World War:

> I remember hearing German planes over head and anti-aircraft guns firing from Kingsway in Derby. Pieces of shrapnel would whistle down, one large piece knocked off a back door at a house in Lodge Way.

Shrapnel was very jagged and heavy and falling from a height certainly had the capability of killing or seriously injuring anyone it hit. Strangely, in all the war histories I've read this has never been mentioned and I've never seen any statistics of persons killed or injured by our own shrapnel although there must have been quite a few. Probably it was all attributed to the bombs.

There was a very heavy raid. We had a gun site near a searchlight battery and they were firing at these Germans. The targets were actually illuminated – the aircraft were illuminated and the ack-ack was going and there was quite a lot of heavy firing; we rushed out to the gate because we thought we heard a German aircraft get hit and one of the engines on fire.

We rushed up to the gate, which was about 15 feet away from our front door, and my dad suddenly grabbed me and shoved me and shouted to my mother, 'Run!'

We did but we didn't know why. The next thing, there was a huge great flash and a spark, which came up from the gate right by us. It was a piece of shrapnel that had come down. Dad had heard it whistling and could hear it heading towards us.

One thing you never thought of, after the ack-ack, say a minute or so afterwards, was how everything would come down – all the bullets they had been firing would start coming down so it was very dangerous to be outside. The next morning I did find the nose cap of a shell in the garden and a big chip out of the path – it was roughly where my mother had been standing, so my dad had probably saved her life.

One evening, Ron and I were carrying a galvanised tin bath full of water back home from his parent's house near Manor House, which was a long way. Then the air raid siren howled its warning! We emptied the water, put the bath over our heads and ran like anything through the dark streets! The shrapnel whizzed all around and one piece struck the bath with a great clang that sounded right through our heads. Then we had to go back and get another bath full.

The third of these accounts concerns just the kind of nosecone of a shell which we have already looked at. Remember that thousands of these were falling every night on London during the Blitz.

The thing which made the rain of shrapnel even more dangerous in many ways than the bombs which exploded on the ground was that their range was far greater and more varied. When a bomb explodes in a built-up area, its blast is limited to a certain number of yards from the seat of the blast. The walls of a house, for instance, might intercept and reflect back the force of the explosion. The same is of course true for an artillery shell which detonates in the air, but once the pieces have been flung out, they continue on long, curving trajectories which, during the course of the thousands of feet which they fall, might carry them for a mile or more. The force of gravity ensures that when they land, they are travelling with as much force as though they had just been flung out by an explosion.

It is strange that the falling shrapnel which caused such injury, damage and death to civilians has faded from memory, because it was universally recognized at the time to be a mortal hazard, at least as much a danger as the bombs which were falling. The collecting of shrapnel by children was mentioned in passing in some of the *William* stories by Richmal Crompton and this might shed light on one possible reason that the nature of shrapnel and the responsibility for the harm it inflicted has been forgotten. The stories which touch upon collecting shrapnel in *William* books all indicate that the children collecting it were under the impression that it was mainly the remains of German bombs or parts of German aeroplanes. This is reinforced by the recollections of adults who were children at the time. For instance, many children sought for the tail-fins from German incendiaries, which were rumoured to be laying around after an air raid.

So far in this book, we have concerned ourselves with the effects of air raids, and the supposed measures used to counter or deter them, in Britain. There are problems with examining the effects of anti-aircraft fire in Britain, because it was almost invariably mixed up with the falling of bombs. The two types of damage are often indistinguishable. On American territory though, there are two perfect examples of the havoc which AA fire could wreak, neither of which are jumbled in with any other kind of explosions. It is therefore to America that we turn in the next chapter.

Chapter 7

The American Experience, 1941–1943

In the Introduction, readers were invited to conduct a thought experiment; to imagine the effects of firing artillery above a city, without the confusing factor of bombs simultaneously being dropped by aeroplanes. We are fortunate enough to have not one but two instances of such a thing happening in real life. In other words, we are able to see exactly what would happen to a modern city if artillery shells exploded above it and also in its streets. The effects are not concealed or confused by other explosions at the same time. Both the cases at which we shall look in this chapter are of American cities which were bombarded by their own forces.

The American armed forces have an unenviable, and fully deserved, reputation for killing both their own troops and those of their allies. Indeed, so familiar are the Americans with this phenomenon that they have adopted various euphemisms to describe it, such as amicide, collateral damage, blue on blue and friendly fire. Throughout the Second World War, the Americans shot down their own aeroplanes and bombed their own side with such monotonous regularity that it became the subject of a rueful joke which circulated among the British forces: 'When the Germans fly over, the British duck; when the British fly over, the Germans duck; when the Americans fly over, everybody ducks!'

American bombers routinely pounded both their own troops and the those of their allies. Even neutral countries were not immune from this hazard. On April Fool's Day 1944, the Swiss town of Schaffhausen was struck by fifty American bombers, which left over 100 people dead. Despite furious protests by the Swiss government, bombing raids by the Americans continued on and off for the next year, culminating in March 1945 with the bombing of Zurich. Pilot error was responsible, but it still gave a terrible impression of American military capabilities.

The Swiss were not allies of America, they were strictly neutral, and so the killing of their civilians in this way cannot really be regarded as friendly fire, more a year-long series of unfortunate mistakes. However, the killing of their own civilians, on American soil, is in another category altogether. It provides us with the perfect example of the damage which anti-aircraft fire could inflict upon a city in which people were just going about their ordinary lives.

The United States has always liked to keep the military forces of other nations as far away from its shores as possible. The Monroe Doctrine declared, as early as the nineteenth century, that America would not tolerate the interference of European powers in the Caribbean or Latin America. On the other side of America from the Caribbean lay the vast Pacific Ocean and this too was viewed as being part of America's sphere of influence. By seizing places such as the Philippines and Hawaii, the United States effectively established a *cordon sanitaire* on their western side. In this way, the American mainland was separated by thousands of miles from any potential enemies.

As part of their policy of keeping any threat far from the mainland, the United States set up a naval base in Hawaii, at a location known as Pearl Harbor, the largest natural harbour in Hawaii, and so named because of the amount of pearls which were gathered there; the Hawaiians called it 'Wai Momi', which means 'water of pearl'. The islands of Hawaii were annexed by America in 1898, at roughly the same time that the Philippines were occupied by American forces, following the defeat of Spain, the previous colonial power. From 1900 onwards, everybody born in Hawaii automatically acquired American citizenship. This included the very substantial Japanese minority, who had come to the islands as labourers. At one point, over 40 per cent of the inhabitants of Hawaii were of Japanese ancestry.

Readers will, it is to be hoped, forgive this little excursion into the history of Hawaii, for it is necessary to know some facts in order to make sense of what happened in 1941 and to understand why our perception of the events in December of that year has become so distorted. At any rate, America saw Hawaii as the perfect location for their main Pacific naval base and Pearl Harbor became the home of an American fleet. It was roughly one and a half miles from Honolulu, the capital city of Hawaii.

Throughout the 1930s, Japanese military adventures in Manchuria and China caused unease in America. The fear was that a Japanese sphere of influence might begin to spread east across the Pacific, until it encroached upon what the Americans saw as their own interests. When the Second World War began and Japan signed a pact with Germany and Italy, the so-called 'Axis', the fear intensified that Japan had territorial ambitions not only in the Far East, but also in the Pacific. Because Japan is an island, with few natural resources, it relies heavily upon imports of raw materials and might be tempted to invade other countries to secure supplies of oil, rubber or minerals. The Americans decided that the best way to curb any imperial ambitions which Japan might harbour about expanding into the Pacific would be to impose economic sanctions. Because of this, the Japanese came to a momentous decision. They would launch a war against the United States.

Obviously, attacking continental America would have been too great an undertaking for the Japanese armed forces and so it was instead decided to cripple American naval power by striking at the fleet anchored in Pearl Harbor. On 26 November 1941 a strike force of six aircraft carriers, under the command of Admiral Nagumo, set sail for Hawaii. The six carriers were supported by tankers, other warships and submarines. In total, more than 350 aeroplanes would attack Pearl Harbor and it was hoped that so devastating would be the damage inflicted upon American naval power in the Pacific, that it would be years before they were once more a force to be reckoned with in the region.

It must be borne in mind that this was a strictly military attack from the air and the aim was to destroy American ships and aircraft. The bombing was carried out not from thousands of feet in the air, with a wide margin of error, but by dive-bombers and torpedo bombers, which flew in low, so that they could deliver their munitions accurately onto their targets. The attack began at 7:48 am on 7 December 1941 and caused a great deal of damage to the ships in harbour, sinking some and crippling others. It was not the hoped-for knockout blow to American naval power though, because the aircraft carriers were at sea and so escaped harm.

Let us look now at the American casualties after this ferocious assault on a nation with which Japan was, technically at least, at peace. Wikipedia is not the best source to consult when one wishes to be sure of facts, but it is certainly the first stop for many people wishing to find things out in a hurry. We shall therefore begin by looking at what many people will learn about the injuries and deaths in Hawaii, resulting from the attack on Pearl Harbor. Here is what Wikipedia told the casual enquirer in the summer of 2018, 77 years after the event:

> Two thousand and eight sailors were killed, and 710 others wounded; 218 soldiers and airmen (who were part of the Army until the independent U.S. Air Force was formed in 1947) were killed and 364 wounded; 109 marines were killed and 69 wounded; and 68 civilians were killed and 35 wounded.

Anybody reading this would assume as a matter of course, that those sixty-eight civilians were killed by Japanese bombs. A little later in the article, there is mention of friendly fire, but this relates only to American aircraft fired on by their own side.

Of course, Wikipedia is not always reliable, so let us look again at the eyewitness account quoted in the introduction. It was written by Elizabeth P. McIntosh, who was working at that time in Hawaii as a reporter for the *Honolulu Star-Bulletin.* She begins the piece by telling us that she was writing seven days after the attack on Pearl Harbor. She describes the scene on the streets of Honolulu on that December day, during the Japanese attack:

> Bombs were still dropping over the city as ambulances screamed off into the heart of the destruction. The drivers were blood-sodden when they returned, with stories of streets ripped up, houses burned, twisted shrapnel and charred bodies of children.

The vivid account of what she saw in the city of Honolulu that morning continues. Remember, this is an eyewitness, somebody who was present that day and was able to describe in detail what the situation was like in Honolulu:

> In the morgue, the bodies were laid on slabs in the grotesque positions in which they had died. Fear contorted their faces. Their clothes were blue-black from incendiary bombs. One little

> girl in a red sweater, barefoot, still clutched a piece of jump-rope in her hand.
>
> Seven little stores, including my drugstore, had nearly completely burned down. Charred, ripply walls, as high as the first story, alone remained to give any hint of where the store had been. At the smashed soda fountain was a half- eaten chocolate sundae. Scorched bonbons were scattered on the sidewalk.

Combining these two sources, the one an eyewitness and the other a modern summary of what is now known about this historical event, would lead to the inevitable conclusion that in December 1941 Japanese aeroplanes bombed Honolulu and killed many civilians, including children. As it happens, this is completely untrue. There is no reason to suppose that a single Japanese bomb fell anywhere near the city of Honolulu that day.

We turn now to the evidence of another eyewitness to the Japanese air raid on Pearl Harbor. John Garcia was an apprentice pipefitter who worked at the naval base. He describes in detail the attack and subsequent confusion. Then, almost as a throwaway remark about something which he clearly thought everybody knew, he wrote:

> There was so much excitement and confusion. Some of our sailors were shooting five-inch guns at the Japanese planes. You just cannot down a plane with a five-inch shell. They were landing in Honolulu, the unexploded naval shells. They have a ten-mile range. They hurt and killed a lot of people in the city.

John Garcia was in Honolulu and knew precisely what happened that day. He pulls no punches and tells the story in a spare but moving way:

> When I came back after the third day, they told me that a shell had hit the house of my girl. We had been going together for, oh, about three years. Her house was a few blocks from my place. At the time, they said it was a Japanese bomb. Later we learned it was an American shell. She was killed. She was preparing for church at the time.

This then is the control sample which we can use when thinking about the Blitz on London and other British cities. Honolulu was a city upon which no bombs fell from aeroplanes and the only casualties and material damage was caused by anti-aircraft fire. By examining in detail what the naval guns did there, we can get a pretty good idea of what they did in British cities.

Honolulu was, as John Garcia said, shelled by 5in naval guns. These were artillery pieces mounted on the warships anchored at Pearl Harbor. The Mark 12 5in/38 naval gun was introduced onto American ships from 1934 onwards and was still in use as late as 2008. There were two versions, the single purpose and dual purpose. The single-purpose gun was only intended for use against surface targets and not aircraft. This was partly due to the fact that its maximum elevation was 35 degrees and also because it was impossible to use time-delayed fuzes with it. In other words, any shell fired from this particular piece of artillery would explode on impact. It was only ever intended that this weapon would be used on targets at ground level.

There was also a dual-purpose version of the Mark 12 5in/38 naval gun and this one could be pointed up at the sky to hit aeroplanes and fire shells with time-delay fuzes. Anti-aircraft shells were at that time, as we have already seen, fitted with miniature clocks, so that the gunner could calculate approximately how high an aircraft was, how long it would take his shell to reach that height and so on. Then, the fuze could be set appropriately and, with a good deal of luck, it might explode near the aeroplane or airship at which it had been aimed. That, at least, was the theory. Of course, in time of panic, for instance when men are under sudden and unexpected attack, they might not stop to fiddle around with setting a fuze in this way. Instead, it is entirely possible that they will just slam the shells into the breech and fire them, without any preliminaries. If so, then any shell missing the aeroplane at which it has been pointed will, if it lands on the ground, explode on impact.

There was a very large number of anti-aircraft batteries around Pearl Harbor and had these been in action, things might have taken a different turn. The army though, rather than the navy, were in charge of the scores of anti-aircraft guns and they were not at all prepared for an air raid. Because so many of the inhabitants of Hawaii were of Japanese descent, the commander of the army garrison, Lieutenant General

Walter Short, was more worried about sabotage than he was of Japanese bombing raids. One of the measures he took to protect aeroplanes from harm was to make sure that they were neatly lined up in the middle of the runways. This meant that they were in plain view and it would be easier to spot anybody creeping towards them and trying to plant a bomb. Unfortunately, of course, this arrangement also made them a marvellous target when the Japanese dive-bombers swooped down onto the airfield.

Despite having sixty mobile AA guns and various other ordnance which could have been used against the attacking bombers, to say nothing of the hundreds of aircraft of their own which could have been sent up to defend the warships anchored in the harbour, the army did almost nothing at all in the defence of Pearl Harbor that Sunday morning. If only the Japanese had attacked just a few days earlier, things might have been very different.

Despite believing that the primary threat to military forces in and around Pearl Harbor came from fifth columnists, Japanese-Americans who might wish to carry out subversive activity on behalf of Japan, Lieutenant General Short conducted regular exercises to ensure that the forces under his command were ready to meet any external threats to Hawaii. For that reason, a seven-day long exercise had begun on 30 November, which included the issuing of live ammunition to anti-aircraft batteries, practising getting fighters into the air as quickly as possible and various other manoeuvres. It was Short's intention that whatever danger might menace the islands, he and his men would be ready to face it.

The week-long exercises staged by the military ended on 6 December 1941, which was of course the day before the Japanese attack on Pearl Harbor. Lieutenant General Short felt that his men deserved a break after all this activity and so he returned the bases to normal, allowing the troops passes to visit Honolulu and generally take it easy. The ammunition for the AA guns was collected and locked away. During the manoeuvres, the aeroplanes had been kept in protected positions, safely hidden away from the supposed enemy. Now that the games had ended, they were all lined up again on the runways, so that they were not at hazard from what Short believed to be the real danger, the traitorous saboteurs whom he thought were buried in sleeper-cells on the islands of Hawaii. These neat lines of planes made a very enticing target for the Japanese dive-bombers when they arrived the next morning.

The situation regarding the defence of Pearl Harbor has been described at some length, because it has great relevance to the Blitz on Britain in 1940–1. The reason for this was that the British, like the Americans, found themselves firing heavy-calibre naval guns at incoming bombers, with catastrophic results. In Britain, the dreadful consequences of firing at aircraft with naval guns was largely disguised by the bombs which were exploding in the vicinity, but this was not the case in Hawaii. In Honolulu, no bombs were dropped on the city from aeroplanes to confuse the situation. All the explosions were from improperly used or defective shells from naval guns.

We have looked at some of the technical specifications of the Mark 12 guns which were mounted on the warships in Pearl Harbor and used to try and shoot down aeroplanes. The British used the 4.5in naval gun on their ships and also as anti-aircraft guns on shore as well, for the same purpose. These may be seen in Illustration 12, which shows a gun of this calibre on Clapham Common and also in Illustration 13, taken on Wanstead Flats in East London. These guns were used in the middle of cities, too. Illustration 4 shows a 3.7in anti-aircraft gun in an anti-aircraft emplacement that survives today in the London docks, at Mudchute. During the war, a 4.5in naval gun was first used at this site, firing its shells above, and sometimes onto, the streets of London.

Even larger-calibre naval guns were used in London during the Second World War. The damage and deaths in Honolulu were caused, as we have seen, by 5in guns. In various parts of London, including in the centre of the city, 5.25in guns were positioned. Illustration 2 shows a pair of these on the top of Primrose Hill in Camden. Just like the American guns at Pearl Harbor, these lobbed enormously powerful shells into built-up areas, with lethal consequences.

One point about naval guns of the kind which were used at both Pearl Harbor and in London to try and shoot down aeroplanes is that the shells which they fired were extremely large. Both the American guns and the British 4.5in guns fired shells weighing 55lbs (24.9kg). The 5.25in guns fired shells weighing much more than this, a staggering 80lbs (36.3kg). The effect of such a shell exploding in the air above a city would be alarming enough, causing heavy chunks of red-hot metal to rain down from the sky, but of course not all of them *did* explode thousands of feet in the air. Many had defective fuzes and others had time fuzes which had not been set, which meant that they would land on a city and explode on impact. It is difficult to visualise the magnitude of explosions, because most of us have little experience of such matters. Perhaps looking at some explosions in recent years will help to show the power of a 55lb shell.

In 2005, four suicide bombers detonated bombs on London's transport system, three in underground trains and one on the top deck of a bus. All were carrying bombs made of roughly 2.5kg of acetone peroxide, a high explosive which is about 70 per cent as powerful as TNT. Germaine Lindsay set off his bomb on a Tube train travelling between King's Cross and Russell Square. The explosion killed twenty-six people. The bomb attack on the Manchester Arena in 2017 used a similar amount of the same explosive and left twenty-three people dead, including the attacker. This gives us a very rough idea of what a bomb weighing 2–3kg is capable of and allows us to compare it with a military shell weighing seven or eight times as much. Let us return now to Hawaii on the morning of 7 December 1941 and see what effect the shells from the naval guns had when they hit Honolulu.

Because the army anti-aircraft guns were not responding to the attacking planes, crews on the warships in the harbour began firing their guns at the incoming bombers. Shooting down an aeroplane in that way, by firing directly at it, as though on a target range, is almost inconceivably unlikely to bring anything down. One can hardly blame the terrified crews though for taking what action they did. Some of the naval guns were not able to be pointed any higher than 35 degrees and the shells for these were simply primed to explode on impact. Even on the dual-purpose Mark 12 guns, which were designed to be used for anti-aircraft fire, the delayed timer on the shells had to be adjusted before they were fired. Since the firing was practically at point-blank range, there would have been little point in doing this. The hope was that the shell would actually strike the plane and explode as soon as it hit it. This meant that all the 5in shells being fired that day would explode with devastating force if they missed their target and came to earth.

Jitsuo Hirasaki was a 48-year-old Japanese-American who ran a restaurant in Honolulu. On the morning of the Japanese attack, he was in his restaurant with his wife and children. A 14-year-old cousin was present, as were seven young men. A 5in shell crashed through the window and exploded inside the building. Jitsuo Hirasaki was killed instantly, as were his three children, Jackie Yoneto Hirasaki, aged 8, 3-year-old Robert Yoshito Hirasaki and Shirley Kinue Hirasaki, who was 2. Their cousin, 14-year-old George Haruyuki Okada, also died. Seven young men, aged between 19 and 27, who just happened to be eating breakfast in the restaurant, were killed as well. Three of them belonged to a Christian youth organization.

Elsewhere in the city, more shells were falling onto the streets, shops and homes. One landed on a house in Kamanaiki Street, killing Barbara June Ornellas and Gertrude Ornellas, who were respectively 8 and 16 years of age, and also 33-year-old Peter Souza Lopes and Frank Ohashi, who was 29. In addition to the deaths, there were many injuries, some of them very serious. A shell landed near a Sunday school and a piece of shrapnel almost severed a boy's arm, which later had to be amputated.

Eighteen months after the end of the Second World War statements were taken from many people in Hawaii, soldiers, sailors and civilians, in an attempt to put together a definitive account of what had happened that day. Here is part of the statement of Mrs Toraichi Kagihara, which was taken on 14 January 1947. It provides an unbearably vivid picture of the situation in Honolulu, as the navy inadvertently shelled the city:

> On the morning of December 7th, 1941, my sister, Mrs Kisa Kagihara, was killed by anti-aircraft shell fragments, which fell thru the basement wall of the duplex apartment which three and her three children and my younger brother occupied at 944 McCully Street.
>
> As Pearl Harbor was being raided, everyone around the neighbourhood were all excited and talks of evacuating the premises were spreading, so my sister were hurriedly packing the necessary belongings of her family upstairs. Her youngest child Elinor, eight years old at the time, tried to be helpful to the mother gathering the things, running from one room to another. In the midst of her packing a shell (presumably fired by our anti-aircraft gun from punchbowl) pierced the side wall of the basement hitting the concrete floor and exploding.

> The concussion was so terrific that my younger brother Harry who had just stepped out of the basement was lifted off the ground from the pressure and he held on to the pear tree which grew near the front step. The exploding fragments flew upward hitting my sister on the leg. Her left leg was broken near the pelvis without any external wound. Elinor miraculously escaped without a scratch, so did Harry. Elinor rushed downstairs to tell Harry what had happened to mother, and with the neighbours' help, rushed her to the hospital, but she probably died on the way to the hospital from loss of blood. By the time Harry returned from the hospital, the house was completely destroyed by fire.

The naval shells continued to bombard Hawaii's capital city throughout the morning, because even when the Japanese had left, many of the sailors were still, quite understandably, jittery and ready to fire at anything or nothing. Coastguards also fired from army anti-aircraft batteries, although by then most of the Japanese planes had flown back to their carriers. Then, in the evening, long after the Japanese had gone, the shelling began again. Aircraft from American carriers had been searching the sea around Hawaii, trying desperately to locate the Japanese fleet. Six planes were running low on fuel and, rather than returning to the carrier, the pilots had been instructed to land on Ford Island, a tiny islet in Pearl Harbor, which had an airstrip. All the forces in and around Pearl Harbor had been warned of the expected arrival of American planes and there was really no excuse for what happened next, other than that it had been an exceedingly tense and trying day. As the planes came into land at Ford Island, heavy gunfire erupted once more and shells began to explode around them. Some of the shells overshot and landed in Honolulu. Five out of the six planes were shot down and three of the pilots killed. It was a terrible coda to one of the worst cases of friendly fire ever seen in American territory, one which had left more than sixty civilians dead from artillery fire from their own side.

The shelling of Honolulu shows us just what can happen if heavy artillery is fired so that it lands in a city. We shall be seeing in the next chapter other examples of this kind of thing which happened in British cities, especially London, at about the same time. Few readers are likely to have heard about this American massacre of their own citizens and there are two main reasons for this. The first is of course that no nation wishes to advertise the fact that it has inadvertently been slaughtering its own people. This explains why official websites and tourist information still to this day give the impression that the people killed in Honolulu and the surrounding district were victims of Japanese bombs, rather than American artillery. There is another reason though for the endurance of the myth and it is that, to put it bluntly, nobody likes to spoil a good story.

Most of the civilians killed during the attack on Pearl Harbor were of Japanese ancestry and had obviously Japanese names. There was something so deliciously ironic about the supposed fact that the Japanese had bombed and killed their own people, that this was bound to become the definitive versions of the events in Honolulu. Something about the idea caught the imagination and tended to show the Japanese, who were by now the enemy, in a bad light. These people were so ruthless that they didn't even care that they were killing other Japanese! It was a neat little bit of propaganda which had the added advantage of serving to disguise what had actually taken place. In a stroke, the bumbling Americans who fired on their own side had been replaced with an enemy who were even merciless to their own people. Little wonder that the fake version of the affair has been remembered in preference to the truth.

Just as the many deaths from artillery fire during the London Blitz at which we looked in the last chapter, the American shelling of one of their own cities is still, 80 years later, not an episode that anybody seems keen to explore. Even modern books steer clear of this embarrassing aspect of Pearl Harbor. Shortly after the millennium, in 2003, the Reader's Digest Association published a book called *WWII: The People's Story.* This was intended to give a fresh perspective on the Second World War. The blurb on the jacket told us that the book, 'brings to life the voices of ordinary people caught up in extraordinary times'. It continues:

> These personal recollections from both soldiers and civilians – many of whom faced dangers as great as those in combat – illuminate the human experience of the war years.

An entire chapter of this book is devoted to the surprise attack on Pearl Harbor and one might think that this would be the perfect opportunity to look at some of those civilians who 'faced dangers as great as those in combat', by seeing how they and their families were blown to pieces while going peacefully about their business that December day in 1941. Not a bit of it! There is no mention at all of civilian casualties. Four of the chapter's fourteen pages are devoted to the USS *Utah*, which was sunk that day by Japanese torpedoes. We are told that 'sixty-four crewmen died on the *Utah*', which was of course fewer than the number of civilians who were killed that day.

Before leaving the subject of the attack on Pearl Harbor, we reflect upon the contrasting casualty figures for the two sides. The Americans lost 2,335 military personnel that day, compared with the 64 Japanese personnel who died. Nearly seventy American civilians were also killed, almost all of them by their own side. The American navy had managed to kill more of their own citizens that day than they had enemy airman and sailors.

The shelling of Honolulu took place from eight in the morning onwards, when most people were up and about. This had the effect of increasing the number of casualties. The next such incident at which we are going to look took place in the middle of the night, when most people were in bed, and so the casualty figures are very much lower. Honolulu was shocking, but it did not take place in continental America. The so-called 'Battle of Los Angeles' was another matter entirely. Not only has it not been forgotten, it has in recent years become a favourite topic of those who believe in flying saucers and alien spacecraft. A Hollywood film has even been made of the incident.

The shelling of Honolulu is a useful case study, for it shows us very clearly the effect on a city of just artillery shells, without the confounding factor of bombs exploding nearby. It gives us some idea of the damage which British artillery was inflicting at that time on cities across the United Kingdom. When Los Angeles was shelled by the Americans in 1942, there was absolutely nobody else involved and all the damage was indisputably the result of 'friendly' artillery fire.

Following the attack on Pearl Harbor, there was a fear in America that the Japanese might be able to strike at the cities of continental America. Reports of approaching aeroplanes and submarines caused people to get jittery and matters were not helped when Secretary of War Henry Stimpson warned the country that American cities should expect to receive 'occasional blows' from enemy forces. It seemed as though he was proved right on 23 February 1942, when a Japanese submarine surfaced off the coast of California and shelled an oil refinery at Santa Barbara. Little damage was done, but the attack certainly served to stoke fears of a forthcoming raid on America by Japanese forces, one which would strike at the West Coast.

Because it is separated from Europe and Asia by two mighty oceans, America has tended to regard itself as invulnerable to attack from either location and the dozen or so shells lobbed at the Californian coast caused great consternation. The following day, naval intelligence warned all units to expect a Japanese attack at any moment. There was a lull of a few hours and then, at about 2:00 am on the morning of 25 February, radar operators picked up what was thought to be an approaching aircraft, a hundred miles or so west of Los Angeles. Anti-aircraft batteries near Los Angeles were put on green alert, that is to say that they were ready to fire on command. It was perhaps inevitable that somebody should claim to see something in the sky and that shooting should then begin.

At precisely 3:06 am an officer in charge of an anti-aircraft gun claimed that he saw a plane flying overhead. He gave the order to open fire on it. Soon, other batteries were joining in, both with 3in artillery pieces and also 0.5in heavy machine guns. Air-raid sirens were sounded, a blackout of the city ordered and air-raid wardens summoned to their posts by telephone. The whole city seemed to be in a state of panic. The alarm soon became self-perpetuating, for as shells exploded high in the night sky, some people staring into the darkness mistook the puffs of smoke for aeroplanes and then opened fire at them with their own guns. What is perfectly certain, and was confirmed by Japanese records after the end of the war in 1945, is that no Japanese plane was anywhere near Los Angeles that night. A total of 1,433 shells were be fired by gun crews over the next hour, as well as an enormous number of machine-gun bullets, until the shooting tailed off at around 4:15 am.

By dawn, it was embarrassingly obvious that there had been no enemy activity at all that night and the various gun crews had all been shooting at shadows. Because the barrage lasted a relatively short time and consisted of fewer than 1,500 rounds, combined with the fact that it took place at three in the morning, nobody was directly injured by the shooting. Five people died, either from heart attacks or road accidents. The most interesting aspect of the thing was the damage done by the anti-aircraft shells and bullets.

The next day's newspapers were filled with photographs of damage to rooftops, cars which had been perforated with half a dozen jagged holes, shattered windows and various other signs that Los Angeles had been subjected to bombardment from the air. This is not really very surprising, because it is estimated that eight and a half tons of scrap metal showered the city in the space of an hour. This was in addition to the shells whose fuzes had been incorrectly fitted and which consequently exploded when they hit the ground. If this barrage had been launched not at three in the morning but, as in the case of Honolulu, in daylight when people were going to work or walking in their gardens, the casualties would certainly have been considerable.

In 1983 the United States Office of Air Force History published a book called *The Army Air Forces in World War II: Defense of the Western Hemisphere*, which contained everything known about the Los Angeles 'air raid'. Their conclusion, which was backed up by official records from America and Japan, together with eyewitness accounts, was summed up as follows:

> A careful study of the evidence suggests that meteorological balloons—known to have been released over Los Angeles—may well have caused the initial alarm. This theory is supported by the fact that anti-aircraft artillery units were officially criticized for having wasted ammunition on targets which moved too slowly to have been airplanes. After the firing started, careful observation was difficult because of drifting smoke from shell bursts. The acting commander of the anti-aircraft artillery brigade in the area testified that he had first been convinced that he had seen fifteen planes in the air, but had quickly decided that he was seeing smoke.

No other explosions of any kind took place in Los Angeles in the early morning of 25 February 1942 and the damage caused to houses, cars and roads shows very clearly the harm that an AA bombardment alone might cause to a city. And this, remember, was all caused by around an eighth of the number of artillery shells fired in a single night above cities such as Manchester and London, night after night for months on end.

Chapter 8

'The Worst Civilian Disaster of the Second World War', Bethnal Green, 3 March 1943

The quotation which forms the title of this chapter is from a commemorative plaque in London. It may be seen in Illustration 19. The memorial marks the spot where more civilians died in the United Kingdom in less than two minutes than on any other occasion throughout the whole of the war. The extraordinary thing about this terrible tragedy is that although the casualties are lumped in with official figures for those killed by bombs and other enemy action, the Germans played no part at all in this particular instance. The British managed the whole thing entirely by themselves.

There were, in the course of the air raids on the United Kingdom during the Second World War, some horrific incidents, some of which claimed more than 100 lives at one time. In 1941, for instance, a bomb struck the Wilkinson's Lemonade Factory in North Shields, killing 107 people. On 18 June 1944, a V 1 landed on the Guards' Chapel at London's Wellington Barracks. A total of 121 people were killed, some soldiers and others civilians. Later that year, on 25 November, 168 civilians died when a V 2 landed on the New Cross branch of Woolworths in South London. Terrible as the loss of life was in these three cases, it was exceeded on 3 March 1943, when more civilians died in a single incident in Britain than at any other time during the war. What is remarkable about the evening which saw the death of 173 people in a London district was that not a single bomb fell that night on the borough where this disaster occurred. The terrible loss of life was caused, as in other cases at which we have been looking, not by enemy action, but rather by the anti-aircraft defences which were supposedly intended to protect the inhabitants of Britain's cities.

Before we find out about the 'worst civilian disaster of the Second World War', it might help to put the incident in context and see what had been happening in Britain since the Blitz of 1940–1. The chief difference between the years of the Blitz and 1942, the year which followed on from it, was the dramatic decline in casualties from German bombs. In 1941 13,431 people had been killed in Great Britain during air raids. In 1942, the figure was just 3,209. In London, the difference between the two years was astonishing. In 1941 6,487 people had been killed in bombing raids, but the following year just 27 died in this way. The mood at the end of 1942 was that German air raids were a thing of the past.

One of the things which we have noticed before is that the fewer deaths during an air raid, the more accurately was the actual cause of death established. When 400 people were killed in one night, it was often assumed as a matter of course that injuries from sharp pieces of metal or blast were from German bombs. When there were only half-a-dozen deaths though, the precise means of death was usually more obvious. This process was at work in 1942, with the fall in mortality rates from air raids, and the figures thus revealed make interesting reading. Before we see what happened during the disaster in March 1943, let us look at one of the air raids which have been well-documented and see how people were actually dying the previous year.

The industrial areas of north-east England were bombed fairly regularly throughout 1942, in contrast to London, where the raids had more or less ended in May 1941. A typical raid took place on the night of Sunday 19 September 1942. The sirens sounded the alarm that night at 9:46 pm and the All Clear a little under two hours later at just after 11:30 pm. In the course of the bombing, the Luftwaffe dropped 20 high-explosive bombs and over 1,000 incendiaries. Brockley Whins railway station in South Shields was hit and the waiting room destroyed, blocking the line for some hours. All the other bombs and incendiaries fell harmlessly on fields and open ground. No injuries or other damage were caused that night by the Germans. The situation was very different though with regard to the effects of the AA guns which had been operating during those two hours.

In Heaton, houses were damaged by falling AA shells in Beatrice Road, Hilden Gardens, Eighth Avenue and Stanley Grove. Two people were badly injured and detained in hospital. In Jesmond, a house in Churchill Gardens was struck by a shell and elsewhere in the town, an exploding

AA shell damaged a water main. In Newcastle, disruption was caused by a supposed unexploded German bomb which landed in somebody's back garden. This turned out to be an unexploded British anti-aircraft rocket. In Darlington, two AA shells exploded, damaging homes and injuring three people with shrapnel. In Oak Grove in West Hartlepool another house was struck by an AA shell. The only fatalities of the night occurred at Jubilee Avenue in New Seaham, where a man and women were killed and two other people seriously injured by an AA shell which landed in the street and exploded. In County Durham, another shell exploded near a house in East Herrington, breaking windows and dislodging tiles from the roof.

This raid described above was far from atypical. Two deaths and five people injured, but not by the enemy. Artillery fire caused all the casualties and almost all the damage to property. The odd thing about all this is that it was no particular secret at the time that AA shells were more of a danger than bombs. It is only since the end of the Second World War that some kind of cultural amnesia has worked to obliterate this unpalatable fact from history, lest it harm our treasured narrative of the Blitz. The matter was even, as we saw in the previous chapter, debated in Parliament at the time.

It is well known that the East End of London suffered a disproportionate number of casualties during the Second World War, due to its proximity to the docks and also the fact that many factories and other strategic targets were located there. In one metropolitan borough of the East End alone, that of Bethnal Green, 527 people were killed during the course of the war. Of this total, no fewer than a third died during the evening mentioned above, that of 3 March 1943. Whether this may properly be described as 'friendly fire' is debatable, but what is beyond dispute is that the deaths were all caused not by German bombs but by British artillery.

By the beginning of 1943, those living in London might be forgiven for supposing that they were no longer in the front line, as they had been during the Blitz. Because so few people were killed during the air raids of 1942, it became clearer than ever what was actually causing those deaths. During one of the raids on London in 1942, which took place on 30 July, not a single person was killed by the bombs which were dropped. The only fatal casualty was a foreign refugee, who was sitting at home with the window open. An anti-aircraft shell flew in through the window and exploded when it landed, killing the man instantly.

The war was certainly beginning to tilt in Britain's favour by the end of 1942. The victory at El Alamein in North Africa, combined with the entry of America into the war against Germany, meant that the ultimate result was no longer in doubt for anybody able to view the situation dispassionately. In keeping with the policy dating from the First World War and developed throughout the 1920s and 1930s, the strategic bombing of Germany had increased throughout the year, there still being some in the RAF who believed that victory could be achieved in this way without the need to send in land forces to fight their way across Europe. This idea was to prove a fatal delusion for, just as in London, the more that the Germans were bombed, the angrier they became and the less inclined to sue for peace. The air raids on their homeland provoked in them and their rulers a desire for vengeance.

On 16 January 1943, over 200 RAF aircraft bombed Berlin, in the first major raid on the city since November 1941. Around 143 tons of high-explosive bombs were dropped, along with 224 tons of incendiaries. The retaliation was swift. The following night, the Luftwaffe attacked London. Between seventy and eighty aircraft dropped almost 120 tons of explosives, together with 213 tons of incendiaries. It had been eighteen months since the last air raid on London and when the sirens sounded, nobody on the ground really knew what to expect. What everybody noticed at once was the enormous barrage which was set up by the anti-aircraft artillery in and around London. Diary entries written by Londoners that night all make mention of the ferocity of the fire directed against the German planes. Newspaper reports also made much of this and treated it as a matter of rejoicing. One article published a few days later said that no city had ever been more heavily defended than was London on the evening of 17 January 1943.

Some of the German pilots had been instructed to bomb specific locations, such as the docks. Others though had simply been told to fly to the areas where there was the heaviest concentrations of searchlights and anti-aircraft fire and then release their bombs there. In fact, many of the planes seemed to have avoided the heaviest fire, which was in Central London and the Isle of Dogs, and bombed instead the less-defended residential areas south of the Thames. A great deal of the damage, and many of the casualties, were to be found in South London boroughs such as Lewisham, Peckham and Wandsworth. A total of 74 people were killed and 233 seriously injured.

With 'only' seventy-four corpses from the raid on 17 January, it proved possible to see in detail how these people had died. This was not always possible during the Blitz, when thousands of people were being killed. Even at the height of the Blitz, in November 1940, most people living in London just slept in their houses as usual, without bothering to take shelter. During the attack in January 1943, this tendency was even more marked. People stood out in the open and watched the bombers flying overhead and the heavy artillery fire which was intended to shoot down the planes. The anti-aircraft fire was very popular with these spectators, some comparing it to a particularly fine firework display. (Later that year, in October, there was consternation when crowds gathered in the streets during an air raid and began shouting good-natured advice to the crews of anti-aircraft guns and generally behaving as though they were at a football match.)

Looking at some of those who died on the evening of 17 January 1943 is a sobering experience. An off-duty soldier and his girlfriend were standing on the Victoria Embankment in the centre of London, watching the shells bursting overhead, for all the world as though they were indeed at a firework display. One of the shells failed to explode in the air, fell to earth and then exploded a few feet from the young couple, killing them both. A public house in Dagenham, not very far from the docks which were a prime target that night, was doing a good trade. Some customers were drinking in the pub, while others stood outside, watching the show. An anti-aircraft shell with a faulty fuze fell on the building, killing four men outright and wounding a number of others. South of the river in Battersea, the caretaker of the Thessaly Road flats was on duty that night as a firewatcher. He too was killed by a shell exploding near to him. In Battersea, on the night of 17 January, an AA shell penetrated an air-raid shelter in the basement of a building before exploding, killing one man and injuring some other people. In Gipsy Hill, a man called J. Ravenal was killed when a shell landed near him, as was a woman standing nearby. Another man was killed at Tooting Broadway. In all that night, twenty-three people were killed by anti-aircraft shells and more than sixty were badly injured. These were the definite casualties from friendly fire, but there were almost certainly others. In short, at least a third of the deaths during that single raid, and more than a quarter of the injuries, were caused by British AA fire.

There is something exceedingly disturbing about such statistics. At the end of this book, we will try and calculate roughly how many people might have been killed by artillery in Britain during the course of the Second World War, but for now it is enough to reflect on the fact that during one raid where the details are known, a third of the fatalities were caused by British fire and not German bombs. When we remember that over 60,000 people were killed during air raids on Britain in the years between 1939 and 1945, it raises the appalling possibility that the number of deaths from friendly fire might conceivably run into tens of thousands. The surprising thing is that it is only in recent years that this has been forgotten; no secret was made of it at the time.

Despite the strict censorship which was exercised over the British press during the Second World War, newspapers were allowed to print details of friendly-fire deaths when they became aware of them. Even provincial papers made mention of the alarming number of casualties caused by heavy artillery, rather than dropped bombs. In a piece about an air raid on London, for instance, the *Derby Evening Telegraph* for 21 April 1943 has a headline which reads: 'MORE INJURED BY SHELLS THAN BOMBS'. A few days later, more Londoners were killed by AA fire and the newspapers even reported the names and ages of the victims. Leading Aircraftman Sidney Scholfield, aged 29, was standing the doorway of a Peabody Building block of flats on Fulham Palace Road on the evening of 23 April. With him was his girlfriend. As they watched the German planes overhead, a 28lb shell landed nearby and killed them both.

As we have seen, anti-aircraft guns were singularly useless as a means of bringing down enemy aeroplanes. Their real value lay in the boost which they undoubtedly gave to the morale of those sheltering from the onslaught of German bombers. They were appreciated more for the noise which they produced than for their ability to hit anything overhead. The ability to generate a great deal of sound could however be a double-edged sword. If it could reassure people, then it could also at times panic them.

Traditional artillery had a number of drawbacks when used to try and shoot down aeroplanes, not least of which was the alarming frequency with which the shells fired up into the air returned to earth and exploded there instead of next to a bomber flying 20,000ft overhead. Even though the government authorized the use of heavy artillery in and around British cities, they knew very well that the purely military value of such weapons was almost nil. It was used by popular demand, not because anybody in the army or air force really thought that it would be a good way of dealing with enemy aircraft. Surely, thought some, there must be a more modern and up-to-date method of taking out aeroplanes? Today, of course, we have guided surface-to-air missiles, which are very effective. These have their origin in the Second World War but their forerunners were anything but effective.

Unguided rockets had been used from time to time by the British armed forces since the Napoleonic Wars. William Congreve's artillery rockets were fired in the general direction of the enemy and could travel thousands of yards. Although not especially accurate, they were useful to fire at a besieged town, enemy shipping or troops on a battlefield. In 1807, they proved very effective during the siege of Copenhagen. Furnished with warheads filled with phosphorous, half the city was burned down by them. The rockets used by the British during the Second World War suffered from the same disadvantages as those devised by Congreve, they were horribly inaccurate, and had it not been for the fact that they were being ardently supported by Winston Churchill, first in his capacity as First Lord of the Admiralty and later as Prime Minister, it is unlikely that they would have entered service.

We touched in an earlier chapter on the idea of the 'aerial minefield', which was supposed to trail wires on parachutes, at the end of which were explosive charges. This system was tried out and found to be ineffective. The means used to launch the parachute mines into the air were so-called unrotated projectiles or UPs. They were called by this name, which was strictly accurate when compared to spinning artillery shells, because it disguised the fact that these 'projectiles' were in fact rockets. Any enemy agents overhearing a reference to 'UPs' would have no way of guessing the nature of the inventions to which it referred. Later in the war the proximity fuze was developed, designed to detonate shells when they were near their target. Again, a confusing name for these was coined: they were called VTs, short for 'variable time fuzes'. Again, the nature of the thing could not be divined merely from the name. Winston

Churchill was the driving force behind the UPs, which were to begin with regarded as a naval weapon. Their development was encouraged by Churchill after he was appointed to the Admiralty after the outbreak of war in 1939.

Batteries of unrotated projectiles were mounted on various warships, including the flagship HMS *King George V*, but they were never popular. The idea was that if the ships were under attack by aircraft, they would use their UP projectors to throw up a trailing screen of wires, which, if any aeroplane ran into them, would swiftly cause an explosive charge to be drawn up and exploded against the body of the 'plane. At their first demonstration at Scapa Flow, precisely the same thing happened as had taken place when the Austrian army used floating balloons against Venice a century earlier. The wind unexpectedly changed direction and the parachutes and their wires became entangled in the rigging of the ship which had fired them. Fortunately, only dummy charges were being used at the time. Later, when HMS *Hood* was sunk in action with the *Bismarck* in May 1941, it was noticed that the UPs on the deck had caught fire and were burning fiercely. The order was given to remove all the rocket projectors from other ships of the Royal Navy.

The rockets used by the navy were 7in diameter and at the same time that they were being developed, experiments were being conducted with a smaller version for use on the mainland against aircraft. This had a diameter of 3in and no trailing wires. Instead, there was a high-explosive warhead, fitted with a rudimentary, and unreliable, proximity fuze. This type of fuze was later replaced with one triggered by the rush of air through the nosecone, as the rocket soared into the air at 1,500ft per second. The unrotated projectiles used as anti-aircraft missiles were approximately 6ft long and carried a warhead weighing 18lbs (8.2kg). The body of the rocket was made of steel tubing, rather like a scaffolding pole, and was filled with cordite. This, incidentally, made these rockets even more dangerous for those on the ground than the anti-aircraft shells which caused so many deaths. The reason was simple. When the warhead exploded, the 6ft-long metal tube which had propelled it thousands of feet into the air, simply plunged to the ground like a javelin. This hazard to anybody below was of course in addition to the usual one of shrapnel, defective fuzes and fuzes incompetently set, so that the warhead exploded at ground level, rather than in the air.

The rockets were first tested against a radio-controlled aeroplane in South Wales in October 1940 and performed very well – so well, in fact, that some observers suspected that the demonstration had been rigged. Be that as it may, it was soon discovered that the UPs, of which Churchill had such fond hopes, were not in the least accurate or reliable. The first projectors had been designed to fire just one missile at a time, but this proved quite pointless. The only way that they would be of any use was if dozens at a time were fired. Then, there was at least a faint chance that one might explode close enough to the target to cause some damage. For this reason, the second and third versions of the launchers for the rockets were constructed so that they could fire a salvo of thirty-six in quick succession. This made a terrible roar, audible for a considerable distance. Millions of the rockets were produced and the launching sites were known as Z Batteries. They were set up in many parts of the country from 1941 onwards, including one in London's Hyde Park. They did not really come into their own until the Blitz came to an end in May 1941.

The government had at first been reluctant to allow people to use London's underground railway system as public air-raid shelters, but gave way in the face of popular feeling on the subject. In addition to the ordinary stations which had been open for years, there was a stretch of the Tube which had been built, but along which no trains had run. This was an extension of the Central Line which was going to run from Liverpool Street Station into the East End and then on to rural Essex. Some of the tunnels which had been dug, those around Gants Hill and Newbury Park, on the very edge of London, were used as underground factories for the firm of Plessey's, which was producing armaments. In October 1941, the newly finished, although unopened, station of Bethnal Green was made available to those who wished to shelter in it at night, during air raids.

Initially, 5,000 people a night slept in Bethnal Green Tube station, but this tailed off during 1942, as air raids became less frequent. By the spring of 1943, only a tenth of that number was using the shelter. On 1 March that year, just 587 people slept at Bethnal Green station. That night, the RAF carried out a heavy bombing raid on Berlin, a fact which was not reported in the British press and on the BBC radio service until 3 March. The news of the raid on Berlin caused great apprehension among Londoners that the Germans would retaliate with a heavy air raid on London.

The anticipation that there would be a heavy bombing raid on London on the evening of Wednesday, 3 March meant, not unnaturally, that many more people than usual decided that the safest course of action would be to spend that night in an air-raid shelter. By 8:00 pm, there were already over 500 people settling down for the night in Bethnal Green station and the underground tunnels stretching away from it. Then at 8:17 pm the air-raid sirens sounded. Those who were already making their way to the station to shelter, speeded up their pace, not wishing to be caught out in the open when the bombs began falling.

Most Londoners were by 1943 perfectly familiar with the sound of Ack Ack guns. They found the noise of the heavy artillery comforting and reassuring, knowing that it meant that their side was hitting back against the Germans. What they could not have known was that a new anti-aircraft battery had lately been set up in Victoria Park, just half a mile from Bethnal Green station. This consisted not of the usual artillery, but was a Z Battery of rocket launchers. The stage was now set for the worst civilian disaster of the entire war.

The unearthly sound of rockets being fired in barrages of thirty-six at a time, together with the resulting explosions in the sky above them, sounded like nothing that the inhabitants of Bethnal Green had heard so far during the war. The greatest alarm of all was caused by the sound of the metal tubes whistling through the air as they headed back towards the ground. This proved utterly terrifying, because the only comparable sound was of bombs falling close at hand and this is precisely what many of those hurrying to the shelter thought they were hearing. Rumours spread swiftly that bombs had actually begun to fall and explode nearby and those who were not yet safely underground began to move faster, anxious to reach safety.

It was a rainy evening and the steps leading down to the shelter were slippery and wet. Just as the hurrying crowd was starting to panic, three buses arrived simultaneously, disgorging more people who were desperately anxious to get to cover. They soon heard the whistling rocket tube falling through the air and the claims that the area was being bombed. These people too surged forward, pushing on those who were already making their way down the stairs to the Tube station.

Hundreds of frightened men, women and children stampeded down a stairway illuminated only with a single 25-Watt bulb, in the hope of getting underground and out of reach of the bombs. There were no central handrails for anybody to grab hold of or lean against and almost everybody was relying for balance upon leaning against the person in front. At a point when 250 people were all crammed onto the stairs, a middle-aged woman carrying a baby stumbled at the bottom of the stairs and lost her footing. Other people tripped over her in the gloom and the press of people from above meant that more people then fell down. Within a few seconds, the stairs were completely blocked with a solid mass of bodies. Just 90 seconds later, 173 people had suffocated. There was only one broken bone, for the others, there were no marks on the bodies, the pressure simply meant that they could not breathe and so died almost at once. Remarkably, the woman who had tripped in the first place and precipitated the disaster survived. The baby she was carrying did not.

A total of 542 people died of war-related injuries in London during the whole of 1943. A third of them were killed in this single incident at Bethnal Green and would certainly not have died had the unrotated projectiles not been fired that night from Victoria Park. It need hardly be added that no German aeroplanes were brought down by the rockets, nor did a single bomb fall that night on Bethnal Green. Given these circumstances, it is probably reasonable to include the 173 men, women and children who were suffocated that March evening as casualties of friendly fire.

Before seeing what else was happening in London on the night of the Bethnal Green disaster, it is interesting to note an urban myth, or rather a series of myths, which have grown up in recent years about this event. As we know, the deaths from friendly fire in Britain were no secret at all during the Second World War, being widely reported in newspapers. It is only since the end of the war and the growth of the precious myth about the Blitz that there has been a tendency to brush the deaths from artillery fire out of sight. This has led to a strange state of affairs where British newspapers during the war actually printed the news of some events more openly than is done today! Consider this article from *The Independent* on 3 March 2018. It is a piece about the tragedy at Bethnal Green at which we have been looking and claims that the affair was in some way hushed up or the facts suppressed at the time. After claiming that a newspaper reporter trying to write about the deaths on 3 March 1943 had his story censored, the journalist writing in 2018 suggests that the whole thing was kept secret for years and the truth only lately revealed:

> Years pass but many survivors wait more than half a century, or until they are on their deathbeds, before letting go of their secret. The wider public is merely informed that Bethnal Green Underground Station has been the unfortunate target of a bombing raid, a direct hit.

The Wikipedia article on the Bethnal Green tragedy makes a similar claim, saying that:

> Among the reports which never ran was one filed by Eric Linden of the *Daily Mail*, who witnessed the disaster. The story which was reported instead was that there had been a direct hit by a German bomb. The results of the official investigation were not released until 1946.

This is all utterly baffling, for we turn to the statement issued the following day by the Ministry of Home Security. Less than 24 hours after the event, this statement contains all the salient information about the disaster. It begins:

> On Wednesday evening a serious accident took place near the entrance to a London tube shelter, causing the death by suffocation of a number of people . . .

The statement goes on to give a most detailed account of the incident, even down to the slightly inaccurate figure of 178 dead. Far from trying to lay the blame on a German bomb, we are told bluntly that 'No bombs fell anywhere in this district during the evening'. It is strange to think that the government statement, reported in newspapers ranging from the *Dundee Courier* to the *Liverpool Daily Echo* less than 48 hours after the event, is more accurate about the Bethnal Green tragedy than the accounts appearing today on Wikipedia or in the national press!

The men, women and children who died at Bethnal Green Tube station on the evening of Wednesday, 3 March 1943 were not the only fatal friendly-fire casualties in London that night. One shell struck the Redhill Infirmary, a hospital in Edgware. It passed through the roof and exploded in a ward containing three old women, one of whom was killed instantly and the other two seriously wounded. In South Norwood, 54-year-old Arthur E. Porter was on firewatching duty. He was killed when a shell landed near him. Shortly afterwards, Alfred Martin was killed near his home in Waddington Way, Upper Norwood, when a shell landed in the road and exploded. Elsewhere in South London, an AA shell came down on top of an Anderson shelter in a back garden. A married couple were sheltering there with their daughter: both mother and daughter were killed by the explosion. Three soldiers manning an anti-aircraft gun were killed when a shell fired by another battery landed on their gun and exploded.

Because the number of deaths during the bombing in 1943 was so low, it is possible to be a little more accurate in distinguishing which were caused by enemy bombs and which by British artillery. This is something which was noticeable too during the air raids of the First World War. When only five or six people were killed, it was easier to distinguish the actual cause of death. When, for example, no bombs fell in an area and a civilian was found lying dead in the street with a piece of metal embedded in his or her head, then it was a fair guess that a piece of shrapnel from an anti-aircraft gun might be implicated. If, on the other hand, 200 tons of bombs have been dropped and 6,000 shells fired, resulting in the death of 500 people, the general chaos makes it impractical to separate out the casualties carefully into those who have died as a direct result of enemy action and those killed by one's own side. What we can say with confidence though is that over a third of the deaths in air raids on London in 1943 were not caused by German bombs.

In the whole of London in 1943, 542 people died during air raids. Just in the two raids at which we have looked carefully, the one in January that year and the other in March, we are able to account for over a third of that figure and see that German bombs played no part in their deaths. In January, 23 people were killed by anti-aircraft fire and in March, 173 people were killed in a borough upon which not a single bomb fell. This gives us 196 out of the 542 deaths in London that year. Those deaths are not the whole story, of course, not by a long chalk. In one raid in October, that same year, four shells exploded in the South London district of Camberwell, killing one man and injuring many others, while in Sydenham, also in South London, a man and his two step-children were killed by an anti-aircraft shell on the same day. At the Dover Castle pub in Westminster Bridge Road, a barrage balloon which had been set on fire by an exploding anti-aircraft shell fell to the ground, killing two firemen. Two more casualties of friendly fire.

Looking at the number of fatal casualties in air raids on London in 1943 and seeing how many were nothing to do with the falling bombs, we reach a shocking conclusion. We know without the shadow of a doubt that at least a third of the deaths were not caused by bombs and can speculate that perhaps another few dozen were attributed to bomb blasts, but were in fact caused by anti-aircraft fire. This suggests that it is entirely possible, and indeed quite likely, that around half the deaths in air raids on London that year were related to anti-aircraft fire.

To be fair to the authorities, it has to be said that many of the casualties could have been avoided if people had behaved a little more sensibly during air raids. Even at the height of the Blitz, there were queues outside cinemas and many ordinary men, women and children, carried on their lives with no regard at all for the falling bombs and artillery shells. By 1943 this disregard had changed and far from being a something to endure, air raids had become almost spectacles to be enjoyed, a little like fireworks displays or football matches. A woman called Vere Hodgson kept a diary in London of what she saw and experienced during the air raids of the Second World War. On 10 October 1943, she wrote:

> Jolly old Wailer set up on Thursday night. This time it was the goods. Gunfire loud and frequent. Searchlights filled the sky and planes caught in them. Lots of people watching. Ladbroke Square gun cracking out. Donned my tin hat — courage returned and I joined the sightseers. All London was doing the same. Shells bursting and amazing fireworks filled the air above us. Went in for the News — then came another wave of bombers. Our bombers were on the way out as the Germans came in — sometimes the searchlights caught one of ours, and sometimes the enemy.

Crowds were gathering out in the open to watch the shells exploding overhead and it can hardly be wondering at that some were struck down by pieces of shrapnel. We have a pretty good idea of what happened in London that night, by looking at the following day's newspapers. The headline in the *Dundee Courier* read, 'AA SHELLS KILL FIVE PEOPLE'. We recall the Home Secretary's words in Parliament in March that year, when he had been asked about this very practice, that of treating air raids as a spectator sport:

> I cannot too strongly emphasise that the public, unless their duties otherwise require, should not neglect the warnings so often given not to remain unnecessarily in an exposed position during an air raid, but should take cover in the nearest accessible shelter, including surface shelter.

Nor were deaths from British artillery fire limited to London. Just over a week after the Bethnal Green Disaster, two men, one of them a firewatcher, were killed on Teesside by an anti-aircraft shell. Throughout the whole country, the low numbers of deaths from enemy bombs allowed the scale of the casualties caused and damage inflicted by the artillery to be revealed. In Parliament and newspaper reports, it was being conceded that AA fire was a serious menace to life and limb.

The delivery of bombs by aeroplanes flying over Britain was coming to an end and with it, the pointless death of civilians at the hands of their own armed forces. Throughout the entire country, just 2,371 people died in air raids in 1943, compared with the 19,918 who were killed in this way in 1941. In 1944, the bombing of Britain in this way would come to an end, being replaced by automated weapons which would drive up the death rate. This time though, all the deaths would be from enemy action and the anti-aircraft artillery would be responsible for none of them.

Chapter 9

The 'Baby Blitz' and the Bombing of France, 1944

As 1944 began, the Blitz had been over for two and a half years and the war against Germany was clearly being won. Europe was still occupied in the main by the Germans though and it was obvious that at some point, an invasion would have to be launched from the British Isles, one which would be very costly in terms of human life. Still, with the Americans fighting alongside Britain and the Soviet Union also on the same side, it could only be a matter of time before Hitler's regime was defeated. The fear of Britain being invaded was a distant memory. In 1940, over 22,000 civilians had been killed during air raids, but these prolonged and heavy attacks had come to an end in the early summer of 1941. There had been some sporadic hit-and-run attacks in 1943, but it was thought that large-scale bombing raids were a thing of the past. Britain and America were free to bomb German cities with impunity, but there was little fear of serious retaliation.

It might have been apparent to the British and Americans that Nazi Germany's days were numbered, but that was not at all how the matter presented itself to the leadership of that country. The Allies had been bombing German cities for some while and Hitler determined in early 1944 to take the war to Britain again. This was to be done by means of a operation codenamed Steinbock. It would be a strategic attack on southern Britain, with the focus, as during the early days of the Blitz, on London. The British knew by December 1943 that something of the sort was planned, because of course they had cracked the Enigma cypher and were able to intercept and decode much of Germany's military communications made via radio.

There were probing flights by small forces of German aircraft from 2 January 1944, but the first proper attack in force did not take place until the night of 22 January. This first raid of Operation Steinbock was codenamed *Unternehmen Mars*, or Operation Mars. Over 200 bombers crossed the Channel and headed across Kent towards London. They were carrying, in the main, extremely large bombs, typically weighing 1,000kg. Navigational errors though meant that few of the planes reached their targets. In the second wave of the night's bombing, only 30 or 40 tons of bombs, out of a total of 235 tons dropped, landed on London. The night was a terrible flop for the Luftwaffe, causing little damage to London other than the deaths of fewer than 100 civilians. Eight days later, sixteen German planes returned to London, but this time nobody was killed and there was no significant damage to property.

We have observed that it feels far better for families grieving for the loss of a relative if they feel that the death of the husband, son or sister was a noble sacrifice, rather than a pointless accident. This state of affairs arose very frequently during the bombing of Britain in the Second World War. Illustration 18 shows a gravestone which mentions the death of a young woman on 22 January 1944, during the first of the air raids which made up what Germany referred to as Operation Steinbock and came to be known in Britain as the 'Baby Blitz'. We see that according to this, 28-year-old Joyce Winifred Rose 'made the supreme sacrifice during an air raid on London'. This is the generally accepted version of the deaths of many who died during German bombing raids at that time and the pleasant and reassuring myth has been passed down to us over the years, virtually intact. A modern website about lost hospitals of London tells us, apropos of the Bexley and Welling Hospital at which Joyce Rose was working as a nurse in 1944, that, 'In 1944 the Nurses' Home received a direct hit by a bomb and burned down. One nurse was killed and three injured.' As far as this goes, it is perfectly correct, but the direct hit on the nurses' home in Bexley was not a German bomb, it was a British shell. The 'Baby Blitz' continued sporadically until May 1944, causing a total of 1,556 civilian deaths. Most of these were caused after the start of the campaign in January. In January itself, fewer people were killed in London by the bombing than died as a result of AA shells.

At the time of writing the news in Britain is dominated, as it has been for some considerable time, by Brexit, the United Kingdom's decision to leave the European Union. The chief players in this drama are Britain,

France and Germany. It is only by knowing the past history of these three nations that the relations between them may fully be understood. From the beginning, Britain's relationship with the European Project has been dominated by the remembrance of things which happened almost 80 years ago. The very admission of Britain to the Common Market, as it then was in 1973, was only achieved after a number of humiliating rebuffs by France, led at that time by Charles de Gaulle. De Gaulle's opinion of Britain's suitability to enter what he thought of as his club, was formed in large part by events in the Second World War, some of which we are now about to study.

In Europe, the first few decades following the end of the Second World War were poisoned by the memory of the destruction wrought by the German armed forces. In Britain, the Blitz and attacks by V weapons caused bitter feelings against the German nation as a whole. In 1966, when Britain beat Germany at football in the World Cup final, the victory was tinged with a revival of wartime animosity and the feeling that Britain had somehow got one over on a hated enemy. This undercurrent of anti-German feeling was not of course limited to Britain. During the occupation of Amsterdam, German soldiers sometimes asked locals for directions. The invariable answer was that their destination could be reached by walking straight ahead. In Amsterdam of course, walking in a straight line for far enough in any direction will end in falling into a canal! This unhelpful advice was still being given to German tourists in the city as late as the 1970s.

One can sympathize with the animosity felt towards Germany by many of those who lived in Britain during the Second World War. It is hardly surprising that when, over a period of four or five years, your country has been subjected to a devastating assault from the air, in which tens of thousands of tons of bombs were dropped on your cities and over 60,000 people killed, one should feel a little jaded about the country which has carried out these attacks. In Coventry, one of the worst-affected cities, 75 per cent of the buildings were destroyed. The British experience of the Blitz is still a potent collective memory and subconsciously colours the relations between Britain and Germany to this day.

France suffered far more destruction from air raids than Britain, about eight times as many tons of bombs being dropped on that country as fell on Britain during the same period, which is to say 1940–5. The destruction of French cities was also considerably worse than anything which befell the British. Coventry may have lost 75 per cent of its buildings, but in some French towns such as Saint-Nazaire, not a single building was left standing by the end of the air raids there. Photographs of some of France's cities and towns show whole districts reduced to rubble, with almost all the buildings destroyed. The percentage of destruction in various French towns makes horrifying reading; 100 per cent of Saint-Nazaire, 96 per cent of Tilly-la-Campagne, 95 per cent of Vire, 88 per cent of Villers-Bocage. These terrible attacks, some of which would almost certainly be classified today as war crimes, were not, however, carried out by the Luftwaffe, but by the RAF and United States Army Air Force. They too were cases of 'collateral damage' or friendly fire, which killed as many civilians as died in the Blitz on Britain.

This book has been mostly concerned with civilian deaths caused by anti-aircraft artillery. Many people though also died during air raids by friendly forces and this, like deaths from anti-aircraft fire, tends whenever possible, to be brushed away out of sight. Nowhere was this situation worse than in France. The mental image which many of us have of France after the D-Day landings in 1944 is of French civilians welcoming their liberators with smiles and throwing flowers to those who had come to save them from the German occupation. The reality is very different, although seldom mentioned today. A large part of France was invaded and occupied by the Germans in 1940 and this resulted, over the next four years, in many civilian deaths. That the German army was responsible for some of those deaths will surprise nobody; the two countries were, after all, at war. The shocking thing though is that tens of thousands of men, women and children were also killed by Britain and America, two countries who were supposedly allies of France and working to save the country from occupation. The worst casualty toll in Britain during the Blitz was that inflicted during the last major raid on London, which took place on the night of 10 May 1941. In a 24-hour period 1,436 Londoners were killed. In France, the highest number of deaths in one day from air raids was more than double this. On 27 May 1944 a total of 3,012 French civilians were killed by bombing. The difference was of course that in the case of Britain, the air raids were being carried out by an enemy. France, however, was being bombed by Britain and America, who were supposedly her staunch allies.

To make any kind of sense of the dreadful number of civilian deaths in France from friendly fire, it will be necessary to look a little at the history of the first year of the Second World War. Britain's traditionally parochial and isolationist perspective often causes people there to view events in France in 1940 only in the context of the evacuation of British forces from Dunkirk, but for the French, that year is notable for seeing the dismemberment of their country.

Although France declared war on Germany on 3 September 1939, the same day as the British declaration of war, nothing much happened for the next eight months, the period of the so-called 'Phoney War'. On 9 April, Germany invaded Norway and Denmark and then, after a lull of a month, a furious assault was unleashed upon western Europe. On 10 May, German forces swept towards Belgium, Holland, Luxembourg and France. In the Blitzkrieg or 'lightning war' which followed, all these countries were defeated. Belgium and Holland were occupied by the German army and France was split in two, with the northern part occupied by Germany and a rump state led by collaborationists established in the south. Because Paris was now in the hands of the Germans, the capital for this supposedly independent French state was established at the spa town of Vichy.

The invasion of France in 1940 posed a great problem for Britain. Apart from the loss of a valuable ally, the entire Atlantic coast of France, including the Channel ports of Calais and Boulogne, was now in the possession of the German army. This was of great significance, because it was from this area that the Germans might launch an invasion of Britain. Crossing the English Channel at this point and ferrying over an army was of course how the previous two invasions of Britain had been carried out, by the Romans in 43 AD and the Normans a thousand years later. That part of France could, from this point of view, now be regarded as enemy territory.

We have already seen the difficulties of carrying out precision bombing. Even in ideal circumstances, landing a bomb dropped from an aeroplane in one particular spot is no easy matter and when a location is heavily defended by anti-aircraft guns and fighter planes, it is all but impossible. There is, under such circumstances, no real difference between the strategic bombing of a purely military target and the carpet bombing of a territory. So it was than as soon as the RAF began to fly over France to attack German positions, it was inevitable that there would also be civilian casualties.

The Channel ports, where the invasion of Britain was being prepared in the summer of 1940, were an early and obvious target for British bombs. For those living in the area, there can have seemed little to choose between the bombing by the Luftwaffe during the German invasion and the bombing by the RAF a few months later. These early raids caused few civilian casualties, but that was to change as France's industrial capacity began to contribute seriously to the German war effort. Just as during the Blitz on Britain, bombing factories, which are legitimate strategic targets, results invariably in the destruction of nearby homes and the death of workers and their families. In practice, air raids against German military bases and French industrial centres both caused casualties among those living nearby.

The government in the part of the country run from Vichy made great capital of the Allied bombing raids, reminding their citizens that it was Britain, rather than Germany, which was the historic enemy of the French people. Reference was made to the burning of Joan of Arc and the battles of Agincourt and Waterloo, to show that these attacks on France were the latest manifestation of a pattern of enmity going back at least five centuries. Allied air raids certainly provided sufficient ammunition to fuel this propaganda campaign by the puppet government in Vichy. In April 1942 the American air force bombed the Renault factory on the outskirts of Paris. The factory had been commandeered by the Germans and was being used to aid the war effort and so was a perfectly proper strategic target. The bombs dropped on the factory though fell all across the area surrounding the factory, including the metro station at Pont-de-Sevre and the Longchamps racecourse. In all, 327 civilians were killed and another 1,500 injured.

Quite apart from the very real strategic aims of Britain and America in bombing targets in France, there was another purpose behind the air raids which were conducted on that country, one which to modern sensibilities might seem more than a little callous. France was used, in effect, as a training ground for Allied pilots. Before new pilots were sent on missions in the heavily-defended skies of Germany, they were sent to bomb French targets, as a way of getting them used to the whole business of carrying out air raids. They were in fact 'blooded' above France and only when they had had the opportunity of practising the dropping of bombs on relatively lightly-defended positions in France were they ready for the tougher prospect of attacking the real target, Germany. That this is so may be seen from the fact that for the first five months of its operations in Europe, from August 1942 to January 1943, the US 8th Air Force only struck targets in France. Once they had become used to the procedure, then they were ready to go over Germany.

There is of course an element of monstrous hypocrisy about all this. We looked in Chapter 3 at the bombing of Guernica and Barcelona by German aircraft, during the Spanish Civil War of 1936–9. The accusation was made that the Germans were using Spain as a testing ground, not only for both new aeroplanes and other equipment, but also as a convenient place to try out the tactics of Blitzkrieg, which would be so successful when used against other European countries in 1939 and 1940. This, it has been, and still is, suggested, was a dreadful way to behave, using somebody else's country just to let your air force practice new methods of warfare. It is open to debate whether this really was what the German Condor Legion were up to in Spain, but it is certainly what the RAF and USAAF were doing in France. There was a good deal of wringing of hands in western Europe in the 1930s about the destruction wrought by bombers on the ancient Basque town of Guernica, but it was greatly exceeded by the damage caused by Allied bombing of some French towns. A specific and horrifying instance of this will show what was happening at that time.

During the First World War Germany made good use of submarines, blockading Britain and trying to starve the country into submission. Because it is an island, Britain is peculiarly vulnerable to such a strategy. Napoleon Bonaparte also attempted a blockade of the British Isles in the early nineteenth century under the name of the Continental System. It was therefore inevitable that during the Second World War, the Germans should try again to strangle Britain in this way, preventing shipments of food, military equipment and troops from the North American continent from crossing the Atlantic. The submarines used during this war did not operate alone but followed a method devised by the Germans, which they called *Die Rudeltaktik*, the wolfpack tactic. They hunted in packs of eight or nine.

When not on patrol the German submarines stayed in what are known as 'submarine pens', vast structures a little like garages. These had walls and ceilings made of reinforced concrete, to protect them from attack from the air. Submarine pens of this sort were to found during the Second World War not only in Germany itself, at Bremen, Kiel and Wilhelmshaven, but also on the French Atlantic coast at Lorient, Saint-Nazaire and Brest. By 1942, submarines operating from these bases were sinking half a million tons of Allied shipping a month and tackling this threat was a top priority. Locating and neutralizing the submarines at sea was not always easy, but it was thought that if they could be attacked in their bases then not only could the submarines themselves be put out of commission, but their facilities on shore could also be wrecked at the same time. The US Air Force was given the task in the autumn of 1942 of dealing with the submarine pens at Saint-Nazaire. This mission would not entail the American aircraft flying above occupied Europe and should provide a relatively safe introduction to future bombing raids against targets in Germany. In fact, America losses were much heavier than expected, but these were as nothing to the effect that such operations had on Saint-Nazaire itself.

During the nineteenth century Saint-Nazaire had grown from being a small village to a large, industrial town. At the time of the American air raids at the end of 1942 50,000 people lived there. This meant that any bombs which missed their targets, which were of course German military installations, had a fair chance of landing on civilians and their homes. The submarine pens were formidable structures, with walls which were 11ft thick and ceilings 16ft thick, made of heavily-reinforced concrete. The engineers who had designed them claimed that they were capable of withstanding bombs of 7,000lbs (3,175kg), far greater than anything which the American air force was using at that time. There were not only submarine pens at Saint-Nazaire, it was also a major hub of the French railway system. For that reason, it was also bombed in order to try and disrupt the movement of military supplies by rail.

The results of the air raids on Saint-Nazaire were, in retrospect, inevitable. Because they were heavily defended by both anti-aircraft batteries and fighters, the American bombers were forced to fly high and release their loads under less-than-ideal aiming conditions. There was inevitably what is sometimes known in military circles as 'spillage', that is to say, death and destruction were not limited to the designated area, but spilled over elsewhere. In Saint-Nazaire, this meant that the homes of the French people living in the town were blown up and those living in them killed. In all, over 500 civilians were killed by the American bombs, more than died at Guernica during the German air raids.

The damage to the town caused by the high-explosive bombs dropped on Saint-Nazaire at the end of 1942 was as nothing when compared with what was to come. Since high explosives had proved ineffective, the decision was taken by the Allies to use incendiaries. For three days in early 1943, British and American bombers dropped leaflets, urging the civilian population to flee the area. This advice was, in the main, heeded. At the end of the three days, the bombers returned in force, dropping not leaflets but incendiary bombs. Most civilians had left the town, but some had remained. These people died when the entire town was burned to the ground. Photographs taken after some of the bombing raids on towns like Saint-Nazaire show scenes of utter devastation, with not a single building left standing. Such images are indistinguishable from those of Dresden and Hamburg, after they too had been subjected to the mass dropping of incendiaries. The difference is of course that Dresden was in Germany, an enemy nation with whom Britain and America were at war. France was supposedly an ally. The destruction of the town of Saint-Nazaire might have been complete, but one place was left unscathed. This was the submarine pens. So solidly built were they, that not only were they not destroyed by the fire-bombing, they are still standing to this day, the only structures in the area from before 1945. The town was razed to the ground and hundreds of the citizens massacred, all for nothing.

It is hardly to be wondered at that there are those in France today who remember with some bitterness the Allied actions against towns such as Saint-Nazaire. This was not though the worst of the actions taken against French territory during the Second World War. The town was levelled, but most of the inhabitants escaped with their lives. Houses can be rebuilt and the death toll ran to hundreds, rather than tens of thousands. It was the year following the attacks on Saint-Nazaire that most of the French casualties inflicted by Allied bombing and shellfire occurred. In Britain, the Normandy landings on D-Day are remembered as an heroic action which launched the liberation of Europe from the Nazis. For France, the case is slightly altered. They recall not only the liberation of their country from the Nazis, but also death and destruction on a scale which dwarfed anything which the Germans had inflicted upon them.

In June 1944, four years after they had been ignominiously chased from France by the German army, leading to the evacuation of Dunkirk, the British army was ready to return. This time, they would not be alone. The Americans had entered the war after the attack on Pearl Harbor and together the two countries felt that they were in a position to drive the Germans from the territory which they had seized and ultimately to march on Berlin itself and destroy the Nazi regime. Modern books about the landings on the French coast at Normandy, which we now know as D-Day, tend all too often to gloss over the appalling number of casualties, both military and civilian, who were killed by friendly fire during the operation. Here are one or two typical quotations from a book published over 40 years later.

The article about the invasion of Normandy in *The Encyclopaedia of Twentieth Century Warfare*, edited by Dr Noble Frankland, tells us that 'heavy air and naval bombardments preceded the amphibious landings'. We are also told that 'The British and Canadians had a bitter struggle to capture Caen . . .'. Conspicuous by its absence is any mention of the fact that although 3,000 Allied soldiers died on the first day of the landings, just as many French civilians were also killed and that they died at the hand of the British and American forces who had come to 'liberate' them. Let us consider first the destruction of the ancient city of Caen.

The British had of course been to Caen before 1944, something which would have been known to the inhabitants of the city. In 1346 Edward III, King of England, seized the city and massacred 3,000 of those living there. He also burned a large part of it to the ground. The British returned 70 years later, this time under Henry V, who also killed some of the people living there. For this reason, it may be assumed that the arrival of another British army in 1944 might perhaps not have been greeted with unalloyed joy. On the first day of the invasion, the British decided that the best way of preventing the Germans from rushing reinforcements to the beachheads being established on that part of the coast would be to demolish the bridges over the River Orne. The American air force was assigned the task of taking out the bridges but, with their customary lack of precision, missed them entirely and instead razed to the ground a large part of the centre of Caen, killing around 600 French civilians in the process.

After the Americans had failed to bomb the correct targets, the British decided to have a go. They too found it easier to hit the city than they did the bridges. And they too reduced to rubble swathes of Caen, perhaps bringing to mind for those living there those earlier visits from the British. By the time that the bombing was finally over, three-quarters of the city had been razed to the ground, combined with the death of 2,000 civilians. As if that were not bad enough, the Allies found that all their efforts had been counter-productive. The fields of rubble made it very hard for the British and American vehicles to advance and also provided perfect cover for the German troops who were defending the city against the Allied advance. It was to be almost two months before Caen finally fell.

To be fair to the Americans and British, they were not only killing French men, women and children with their air raids. They were also, at about the same time, accounting for many of their own soldiers in the same way. Seizing and holding the Normandy beaches had proved to be the easiest part of the invasion of Europe. The hope had been that once they saw the strength of the united British and American forces facing them, the Germans would crumble and perhaps flee in terror. They did not. They dug in and prevented the Allies from breaking out of the beachheads and sweeping into the open country beyond the coast. Having learned nothing from the failed tactics used at the Battle of the Somme during the First World War, the Allies decided that the best way of crushing and demoralizing the troops facing them would be to pound them mercilessly with high explosives. If enough bombs and shells were used, then the Germans would either be killed or emerge from their shelters as gibbering wrecks, incapable of opposing the advance of the Allied forces. This did not work in 1916 and it did not work in 1944 either.

The Americans, as we have seen, have never had a very good reputation where bombing from the air is concerned. They seem to have an uncanny knack for killing their own troops as readily as those of the opposing side. Despite this, a plan was formulated that would see the American air force delivering hundreds of tons of bombs onto the German lines near the town of Saint-Lô, where the American troops were being held up by stiff resistance from the Germans. The only difficulty was that this would require surgical strikes from the American planes, because the two sides were so close to each other. Operation Cobra, as it was called, was felt to be vital. If something was not done, then the Allies would never be able to leave the area of their initial landings and move out into the open countryside beyond.

The aircraft which were to be used for the precision bombing of the German positions were 1,584 B-17s and B-24s, and the heavy bombers would be flying at 15,000ft. This was the kind of bombardment which was traditionally carried out by artillery, which could of course be more accurately aimed. The Americans though were growing impatient. It was approaching the end of July, almost eight weeks after the Normandy landings, and they were still stuck a few miles inland. They simply couldn't understand why they were unable to advance further.

Even before the bombing began, there were those who could foresee disaster. The gap between the American and German lines was so narrow, only a mile or two, that it would be almost impossible to achieve the desired accuracy. The senior officer who demanded the raids, General Omar Bradley, simply could not understand why the US air force seemed so determined to put problems in his way. His rank meant that ultimately, he was bound to have his own way and the first bombing raid took place on 24 July 1944.

We have already seen many instances of the inability of heavy bombers to pinpoint any particular target with precision when flying thousands of feet above it and that alone was enough practically to guarantee that things would not proceed according to plan. The special instructions issued to the pilots and bomb aimers sealed the fate of the American troops on the ground. These were that the lead bombardier in each group should release his bombs onto the target and that the other planes should simply follow his lead. It goes without saying that if the first bombs went wide of the mark, then so would all the others in that particular group of aircraft. It was little short of a miracle that only twenty-five American soldiers were killed by the bombing that day.

One of the worst friendly-fire incidents involving Allied troops now unfolded with all the inevitability of a Greek tragedy. The omens for the full-scale bombing, which was to take place on 25 July were anything but auspicious. For one thing, the cloud cover was lower than expected, at 14,000ft. This meant that the planes would be flying at a different height from that which had been planned and this in turn meant that all the calculation relating to the optimum time to release their loads would have to be carried out again. A cloud of smoke also obscured much of the ground, making it very difficult to spot landmarks. Despite this, the order was given to go ahead. Over 4,000 tons of bombs were dropped, with of course the intention of systematically obliterating the German defences.

Just as during the previous day's attack, two of the lead bombardiers misjudged their positions and released their bombs early. And also, just as on the previous day, the aeroplanes in their group followed suite, bombing not the German but the American lines. The 30th Infantry Division, which had borne the brunt of the friendly fire the day before, was hit again, with the loss of sixty-one men. In all, 111 American soldiers were killed by their own side that day, including the highest-ranking American soldier to die in Europe during the Second World War, General Leslie McNair. Eyewitness accounts of the effect of the bombing by their own planes are almost unbelievably gruesome. One man wrote:

> My outfit was decimated, our anti-tank guns blown apart. I saw one of our truck drivers, Jess Ivy, lying split down the middle. Captain Bell was buried in a crater with only his head visible. He suffocated before we could reach him.

Apart from the terrible self-inflicted casualties, the whole business bore an uncanny similarity to the attempt during the First World War to crush the Germans with overwhelming explosive power and then simply walk up to the demoralized and bewildered survivors to seize their positions. It didn't work on the Somme in 1916 and nor did it work in Normandy. The Germans had, unlike the Americans, dug in well in foxholes and as soon as the barrage was over, they just came out of their hiding places and began machine-gunning the approaching American troops.

The bombing of Caen had largely demolished the town and caused thousands of deaths. A similar fate befell Le Havre, three months after D-Day. There though, the destruction was even more comprehensive than it had been at Caen. Illustration 17 shows Le Havre after France's allies had finished with it. This could easily be a photograph of Hiroshima after the dropping of the atomic bomb: the ruin is complete.

By August 1944, Paris had been liberated and much of France was no longer under German occupation. Le Havre, a major port in Normandy, which lay on the estuary of the Seine, was still in German hands. The German army knew that a battle would soon take place for control of the town and, to their credit, advised civilians living there to leave for safety. Few people though were inclined to abandon their homes and become refugees. They knew that with Paris in Allied hands, it could be only a matter of time before the Germans were themselves forced to flee from France. On 3 September, the British army, commanded by General Crocker, surrounded Le Havre and laid siege to it. Word was sent to the Germans that now might be a good time for them to surrender, an offer which was peremptorily refused. To reduce casualties on their own side, the British decided to bomb the town and see if that would break the German resolve.

On 5 September, 350 British bombers flew over Le Havre, dropping a combination of high-explosive bombs and 30,000 incendiaries. Every building in the centre of the town was blown to pieces and set alight. Ironically, the only structure which was left intact by the end of the day was the solidly-built memorial to the 1914–18 war. The following day, six waves of bombers dropped nearly 1,500 tons of bombs, together with another 12,500 incendiaries, flattening and reducing to ash eastern part of the city. On 12 September, the Germans surrendered and Canadian forces entered the town. Le Havre had been bombed before by the Allies, in 1941, and civilians had been killed on that occasion too. In total, bombing by their allies had led to the deaths of over 5,000 of the inhabitants of Le Havre by the time the war ended.

The question which is perhaps being asked at this point by readers is why they have never heard about any of this. Even modern sources such as Wikipedia underplay the dreadful events which led to such massacres. After all, carpet-bombing a city in this way and turning it to a wasteland of rubble and ash would certainly be treated as a war crime, and yet nobody, even the French, appear to want to talk about this. What would a young person, eager to find out about the history of Le Havre find, for example, if he were to read the Wikipedia article on the town? Merely this:

> Largely destroyed during the Second World War, the city was rebuilt according to the plans of the architect Auguste Perret between 1945 and 1964. Only the town hall and the

> Church of Saint Joseph (107m high) were personally designed by Auguste Perret. In commending the reconstruction work UNESCO listed the city of Le Havre on 15 July 2005 as a World Heritage Site.

'Largely destroyed during the Second World War . . .', with not the least mention of who or what it was which did the destroying! The answer to this baffling silence on the subject of a series of war crimes is rather curious.

The Vichy regime which was set up in southern France after the German invasion of the country in 1940 was pro-German and anti-British. When the British began bombing targets in the occupied part of France, the Vichy propaganda machine reminded their citizens of the historic enmity which had existed for centuries between Britain and France. This was a popular prejudice which was not difficult to stir up and not a few people in France began to regard the Allied aircraft which were bombing their country as the enemy. A direct line was drawn between the modern situation and such events as the execution of Saint Joan by the British, 500 year earlier.

After the liberation of France by the Allies in 1944, a wave of fury against all those who had collaborated with the Germans or even been part of, or associated with, the Vichy government swept the nation. It is estimated that as many as 9,000 summary executions were carried out in the first months after the liberation of suspected traitors and those thought to have had dealings with the Germans. A natural consequence of this was that nobody wished to be heard supporting any of the views expounded by those who had been in charge at Vichy. This is hardly surprising, since the government there had been complicit in, among other things, the deportation of 76,000 Jews to the extermination camps in Poland. Since one of the things that Vichy had been so vociferous in denouncing had been the Allied bombing raids against targets on French soil, this too became a taboo opinion to hold. At a time when thousands of people were being hunted down and shot on the merest suspicion of having either collaborated with the Germans are supported the Vichy regime, it is not hard to see how anxious people must have been in the aftermath of the occupation not to be heard parroting pro-Vichy sentiments.

Avoiding the topic of the friendly-fire massacres of French civilians was a habit which lingered on long after the fear of being brought to trial as a collaborator had ended. However, although nobody spoke of such things out loud, any nation which has had over half a million tons of bombs dropped on it, killing over 60,000 civilians in the process, is bound to harbour some resentment against those responsible. This was certainly the case with Britain, many years after the Blitz ended and it happened in France too.

It must always be borne in mind that it was not just Britain but also America which caused so much death and destruction to France and this has had a malignant influence upon British relations with Europe after the end of the Second World War. When, in 1961, Britain first tried to join the European Union, or Common Market as it was then called, the request was firmly rejected by the then leader of France, Charles de Gaulle. The reason for de Gaulle's refusal was simple: he believed that Britain was not truly committed to the idea of being a part of Europe and preferred to be part of the American sphere of influence. It was not until 1973, nearly 40 years after the events which followed the Normandy landings, that Britain finally entered Europe. With the row over Brexit, of course, old tensions have resurfaced and in recent years the French have become a little less shy of mentioning the British role in the bombing of their country. It might be suspected that if and when Britain finally withdraws altogether from the European Union, there will be even less reticence on this subject and the friendly-fire incidents at which we have been looking in this chapter will end up being part of mainstream history, rather than being hushed up as something both nations would rather forget about.

Chapter 10

A Military Development as Important as the Atom Bomb

During the so-called 'Baby Blitz' in the early part of 1944, civilian deaths from anti-aircraft fire were still alarmingly common, killing more people in London during January of that year than were killed by German bombs. By the end of the year though, such deaths had almost entirely ceased. Today, deaths from this cause are all but unknown. The only people to die on the ground these days from anti-aircraft fire are those executed in this bizarre way by the regime in North Korea. A newly-designed secret invention, first tested in 1942, both hastened the end of the Second World War and also revolutionized modern warfare. It also put a stop to inadvertent civilian casualties from anti-aircraft fire.

By the 1930s some of the ideas appearing in the novels of H.G. Wells had proved astonishingly prescient. Perhaps it was this which prompted the British government to take seriously the idea of a death ray, one capable of destroying enemy aircraft from a great distance, as well as soldiers as they advanced across a battlefield. In 1898, Wells had written the following description of just such a weapon:

> Whatever is combustible flashes into flame at its touch, lead runs like water, it softens iron, cracks and melts glass, and when it falls upon water, incontinently that flashes into steam.

Imagine something like this being directed against aeroplanes heading towards Britain, intending to bomb cities. A ray of this kind would enable the defenders to stop them above the Channel, before they even reached the coast of Britain.

Although various famous inventors, Nikolai Tesla for example, tinkered with the idea of a death ray, the technology of the time was not sufficiently advanced to make such a thing practical. This left the field open for various confidence tricksters, who set out to try and solicit money from both private investors and governments, promising that a breakthrough was imminent and that only a little more capital would enable the development of this, the ultimate weapon. One such person was a British man called Harry Grindell Matthews.

In the years before the First World War Grindell Matthews founded the Grindell Matthews Wireless Telephone Company, which promoted mobile phones. It was a visionary project which raised a good deal of money for the man running it, but which collapsed in 1914. After the end of the war in 1918, Grindell Matthews emerged as the inventor of a ray gun which would apparently make war impossible. The idea was that ultra-violet light would ionise the molecules making up the atmosphere, so allowing them to conduct electricity. Then a huge charge of electricity would be fired along the ionised air, killing men and causing the engines of aeroplanes, tanks, ships and cars to explode. The only slight difficulty was that a little more money was needed to perfect this wonderful device. Both the British and French governments showed interest in Grindell Matthews' invention, but in demonstrations it proved impossible for the 'death ray' to do more than stall a motorcycle engine a few yards away. This was seemingly the limit of its power. The British Air Ministry though was still intrigued by the idea and offered the sum of £1,000 to anybody who could, under controlled conditions, kill a sheep 100 yards away with any kind of ray weapon.

The £1,000 reward spurred on research into radio waves as a useful means of waging war, but led ultimately in quite a different direction. It was discovered that rather than blowing up aeroplanes, they could actually be bounced off them and the echoes detected from many miles away. In this way, radar was developed, which was to prove of such crucial importance during the Battle of Britain. Towers 300ft high were built along the English coast and these were able to detect aeroplanes heading across the North Sea or English Channel towards Britain. It was this network of radar stations, known as Chain Home, which gave the RAF an edge during the Battle of Britain in 1940. During the Second World War, sets became small enough to carry on board fighters, which also was a huge advantage at night.

The development of radar led in turn to one of the most significant inventions in warfare for many decades, something which was at the time thought to be comparable in importance to the atomic bomb upon which British and American scientists were working at the time. The United States was of course Britain's ally during the Second World War and so it was natural that the British should pass on any inventions which might prove useful for military purposes. The cavity magnetron, which was an enormously powerful device for generating the radio waves necessary for radar, was one such invention which was sent to America in 1940. Another was a means of using radar to detonate bombs and shells when they were a pre-determined distance from their target. We have seen that anti-aircraft fire before and during the Second World War was woefully ineffective. The US Navy had for some time been demanding that somebody design a means of exploding anti-aircraft shells close to the aeroplanes at which they were fired. The dreadful experience of Pearl Harbor, when the navy achieved the dubious distinction of killing more of their own citizens than they did enemy attackers, had reinforced the need for some method for ships to defend themselves against dive-bombers. For the British, a reliable method for preventing AA shells falling back to earth and killing one's own citizens was also of great interest.

The proximity fuze, which the British did not possess the resources fully to develop themselves during the war, consisted of nothing more than a miniature radar set which could, by bouncing radio waves onto any nearby objects, detect the presence of anything large enough to be an aeroplane, ship or indeed the ground. It sounds simple, but the practicalities of building such a device were formidable. The stresses to which an electrical gadget are subjected when fired from a heavy piece of artillery are very great. Not only sudden acceleration, but also the spinning round as the shell passes along the spiral curves of the rifling in the barrel. The principle of the proximity fuze was simple enough, but the technicalities of the thing took years to perfect.

In an earlier chapter, we looked at the attack on Pearl Harbor in 1941. When firing at the Japanese aircraft attacking them during the attack, the sailors had known that the shells they were firing were passing close enough to the planes to destroy them, if only they had exploded at the right time. The proximity fuze promised to make this possible. It could be set to explode when it was between 6 and 30ft from a target. One of the first field tests of the new fuze took place on 13 August 1942.

It was the US Navy which had been agitating for some kind of proximity fuze to fit to its 5in shells and so it was from one of its ships which the first successful test of the new system was made. The cruiser USS *Cleveland* was supplied with some of the new shells and two radio-controlled drones were sent up and flown near the ship, to simulate enemy aircraft. The drones had survived many previous tests without mishap. The odds of a shell actually hitting them were almost zero and so the observers were struck dumb when the first two shells fired blew both drones to pieces. The tests were scheduled to run for two days, but since the relevant department of the navy owned only two drones, nothing more was done for that day. By the morning of the next day, a third drone had been located and this was launched near the *Cleveland.* This time, the first shell missed, but the second one exploded near the drone, destroying it. The proximity fuze had proved its worth.

To begin with, shells fitted with proximity fuzes were provided only to the navy. The reason for this was simple. It was such an enormously important advance in military technology that it was felt that it must at all costs be prevented from falling into the hands of the Germans or Japanese. If one malfunctioned and fell into enemy hands, then it might prove possible for the Germans or Japanese to reverse-engineer a version of their own. Worse still, they might find a way of developing a defence against the proximity fuze. Shells fired at sea would, if they should happen to malfunction, fall into the water and disappear from sight. On land though, such a shell might conceivably fall into the hands of the enemy.

During 1943, the proximity fuze was used to great effect by American ships fighting against the Japanese in the Pacific. Previously, dive-bombers could attack ships of the US Navy with a good chance of evading the anti-aircraft guns. The proximity fuze tipped the advantage in such encounters in the direction of the Americans. So successful were the Americans in bringing down planes which were attacking their ships, that it has been suggested that the famous Kamikaze planes were a direct response to the difficulty which the Japanese were now having in getting close to American vessels. It was to no avail though, for the proximity fuze was just as effective in bringing down planes piloted by suicidal fanatics as it was in dealing with more conventional attacks on shipping.

Because of the secrecy surrounding the proximity fuze, it was never mentioned by name but rather referred to as a VT or variable time fuze. This was to stop the Germans realizing what had been developed and perhaps spurring them on to acquire similar technology themselves. When, during the invasion of Sicily in 1943, a shell failed to explode and ended up on dry land, a special team was despatched to locate it and make sure that it did not fall into the wrong hands. It was in the second half of 1944 that the proximity fuze became crucial to the defence of Britain.

In the early hours of 13 June 1944, four explosions took place in south-east England. Each blast was caused by a ton of explosives and three took place in open farmland in Kent and Sussex. One of the explosions though was near a railway bridge in the East London district of Bethnal Green. This killed six people and damaged many houses. Illustration 20 shows the plaque on the railway bridge in Grove Road which marks the spot where the first V 1 landed in London. There were various stories floating around about what had caused the blast in London, because there had been no air-raid warning, nor had any German bombers passed overhead. Rumours were rife about a crashed aeroplane, but the truth was revealed a few days later, when seventy-three unmanned aircraft, each with an enormous warhead, struck London. The flying bombs which became known variously as 'buzz-bombs' and 'doodlebugs' had appeared on the scene in the last and, to some, most terrifying phase, of the aerial attacks on Britain.

In Germany, the new weapons were known either as FZGs, short for *Flakzielgerut 76* or *Vergultungswaffe Eins*. The first designation translates roughly as 'anti-aircraft targeting device'. Just as with the British, when they used the term 'unrotated projectiles' for the anti-aircraft rockets, the aim was to disguise the true nature of the things and ensure that anybody hearing about FZGs would not really know what they were. The other expressions used for the flying bombs, *Vergultungswaffe Eins*, means 'Vengeance Weapon One', and so it was that they became known commonly as V 1s. The V 1s were primitive cruise missiles. Guided by a gyrocompass, they came without warning at random times. No defence appeared possible against these robots and the fact that they operated without human agency struck many people as uncanny and worse than the bombers which had pounded London during the Blitz. There was something inhuman about this new menace.

Although the government had known for some time about the existence of the pilotless aircraft, even once they began to strike England, nobody had any clear idea of how to deal with them. To begin with, they were fired on by both fighters and also AA guns. Since the V 1s were, at least to begin with, aimed at London, this meant that any which were shot down by anti-aircraft guns in and around London tended to fall on the city itself – hardly an ideal solution. More than that, fighters trying to shoot down the V 1s found themselves also being targeted by AA fire. Since radar could give some warning of the approach of the 'doodlebugs', one idea which was mooted was to maintain a constant curtain of exploding anti-aircraft shells along the eastern approaches to London, whenever V 1s were heading in that direction. This was at first thought to be better than nothing and, just as in the Blitz, likely to show the populace that something was being done to protect them. However, a few rough calculations soon showed that such a strategy would be likely to kill far more people than simply doing nothing. Already that year, anti-aircraft shells had killed more civilians in London in January than had been killed by German bombs and the prospect of thousands more crashing down on the city, along with all the V 1s which they might shoot down, was an alarming one.

The idea finally seemed to be sinking in that artillery barrages over a big city were likely to be lethal to those living there and so the decision was taken to try and stop the V 1s long before they reached London. The AA guns were moved away from the city and set up at first on the North Downs. This did not work very well, because fighters were still chasing the missiles and being menaced in turn by the defending guns. For this reason, the AA guns were moved to the coast. A huge stretch of the coast of southern England, between St Margaret's Bay in Kent and Cuckmere Haven in Sussex, became essentially what we now call a 'no-fly' zone for Allied aircraft. This zone stretched out to sea for 10,000 yards as well. Anything at all which ventured into this area was ferociously bombarded with AA fire. Considering the success rate for shooting down aeroplanes since the war had begun, this alone would have been unlikely to alter significantly the number of V 1s landing on London, but by this stage of the war, it was time to lift the veil of secrecy which had until then stopped the existence of the proximity fuze from becoming generally known.

Side by side with the British artillery positions whose aim was to shoot down the incoming missiles were American guns, working to the same end. The Americans were equipped with 90mm guns and as soon as the British saw them in action, they were astonished at the apparent accuracy displayed by the American gun crews. The Americans were already used to using shells fitted with the new fuzes, but when first seen in action by the men firing British 3.7in guns, the results seemed to be little short of miraculous. One Home Guard crew, used to firing thousands of shells before actually hitting a V 1, watched an American team set to work. With just eight shells, the Americans brought down four V 1s. Used to the strict secrecy surrounding the proximity fuze, the American troops refused to explain the real reason for their accuracy, claiming when asked by the Home Guard gunners that their success rate was due to the fact that those manning the guns were from Tennessee and were well-versed in the use of rifles!

Shortly after the Americans began firing at the V 1s, the British army was allowed to know about the great secret and supplies of shells fitted with proximity fuzes were supplied to all anti-aircraft batteries. The kill-rate improved dramatically. To begin with, just under 17 per cent of the missiles had been shot down, but once the new shells had been distributed, this rose to an almost incredible 80 per cent. Of course, the gun-laying radar units helped a lot, but it was the proximity fuze which really won the day.

There is a sting in the tale when we read about the amazing success of the proximity fuze in tackling the flying bombs and preventing them from reaching London. Just as some of the means of defence during the Blitz in 1940 and 1941 had the effect of protecting Central London at the cost of more bombs falling on the eastern suburbs of London, so too with the V 1s. This time though, the devastation of working-class districts rather than Central London and the West End was a deliberate and cold-blooded decision taken by the government.

The Germans had calculated precisely where their missiles would land. They were all calibrated to be aimed at Buckingham Palace. Even if they missed the palace, they would be likely to land in Westminster or prosperous parts of London such as the West End. The accuracy of the missiles can be seen when we recall that on 18 June 1944, just a few days after the appearance of the flying bombs, one landed on the Guards' Chapel at Wellington Barracks, only a stone's throw from Buckingham Palace. One hundred and twenty-one people died in that one incident. One V 1 actually landed in the grounds of Buckingham Palace, destroying a summerhouse and damaging the King's tennis court. If those missiles which did manage to get past the AA guns on the coast continued to fall on Westminster, then not only Buckingham Palace but also the government offices in Whitehall and various other important locations might be damaged.

German spies had landed in Britain after the declaration of war and most had then been swiftly captured by the police and intelligence service. Some of them were tried and then hanged under the wartime regulations, but others were offered the opportunity to save their lives by changing sides. These men were kept in custody and given false and misleading information to transmit to their superiors in Berlin. Because the V 1s were being so accurately targeted on Central London, it was thought that it might be possible to divert them away from there by persuading those involved in setting their coordinates that they were veering off course. Vivid 'eyewitness' accounts were accordingly compiled and then given to the double agents to send by Morse code transmitters to their handlers back in Germany. These consisted of detailed descriptions of the devastation inflicted by the flying bombs on sparsely inhabited parts of north London, some miles from the places where the V 1s were actually coming down. The Luftwaffe had already made photographic reconnaissance flights over London and recorded the damage to locations in the centre of the capital, but surprisingly, the spurious reports from the spies were given more credence that the actual photographs.

Adjusting the coordinates to compensate for the supposed tendency of the V 1s to veer to the north meant of course that whereas before they had been landing right in the heart of London, just as the Germans hoped that they would, they now began striking a few miles south, on the other side of the Thames. This is why Croydon, on the very southern fringe of London, was the district most heavily hit during the V 1 attacks. Just over 10 per cent of all the flying bombs which managed to get through the defences landed in this outer London borough. The South London boroughs of Croydon, Lewisham, Bromley, Bexley and Orpington were known collectively as 'doodlebug ally', because so many V 1s landed there. A month after the first V 1 had struck London, over 200,000 homes in 'bomb ally' had been damaged by the 'doodlebugs'. At least though, the scourge had passed from the West End and Whitehall.

Friendly-fire casualties in Britain from anti-aircraft fire ended when the Germans stopped sending over aeroplanes to drop bombs and turned instead to cruise and ballistic missiles. This coincided with the widespread use in Britain of the new proximity fuze. Although friendly-fire casualties from AA fire were still high in the early part of 1944, they had dropped off to almost zero as soon as the V 1s started arriving. The last enemy attack on the British mainland came as late as 29 March 1945, when a V 1 was launched at the country from a Heinkel bomber, but by that time there had been no injuries or deaths from anti-aircraft shells for almost a year.

Endword

The story of the Blitz outlined in this book has been very different from the familiar narrative which we learned about at school. This is the thing though about real history, it is messy, confusing and makes little sense until we have arranged it into neat episodes and easily understood concepts. For that reason, we often fasten historical narratives onto a metaphorical Bed of Procrustes and either stretch them or lop bits off until we are able to fashion them into pleasing fables. Plucky little Britain, standing alone against the might of Nazi-dominated Europe is a good example of such a myth.

We have traced the story of aerial bombardment and anti-aircraft fire over a period of just under a century, from the balloon bombs launched by the Austrian army against Venice in 1849 to the last V 1s and V 2s which fell on Britain in 1945. The particular subject of this book has of course chiefly been civilians killed by artillery fired by their own armed forces. We have been able to establish very accurately the number of American civilians who died in this way, perhaps sixty-five in Honolulu and another five in Los Angeles. Finding corresponding figures for Britain has not proved so straightforward.

Deaths from artillery fire in Britain between 1940 and 1945 have been hidden by two principal causes, the one physical and the other psychological. Physically, the casualties of British artillery at that time have been hidden by the simultaneous deaths of the thousands of people killed by enemy bombs. When over 400 people have died in one city in the course of eight hours or so, it is not always practical to sort the victims into neat categories, according to whether the masonry which fell on their heads and killed them was dislodged by an exploding shell or the effects of a bomb. The injuries in either case are identical and it is kinder to the families during a war to cast them as heroic martyrs, rather than victims of a blunder.

The psychological aspect of the thing is that unless one is being deliberately iconoclastic, then there is little point in writing anything which contradicts the myth of the Blitz. It is this which accounts for the fact that even today, writers tend to steer clear of the subject of friendly-fire casualties. The most which is said in the majority of books, when the subject is touched upon, is that more civilians were killed by AA fire than by the Germans, which is incontrovertibly true but understates the case dramatically. Let us look at two extremes and see if we can work out a maximum and minimum figure for the fatal casualties among British civilians caused by their own artillery during the Second World War. We will start with a shocking assertion made by one of the scientists who worked upon the proximity fuze, which we read about in the last chapter.

Much of the early work on the proximity fuze which was to prove of such inestimable value to the Allies was carried out at Cambridge University's Cavendish Laboratory. The need for the proximity fuze was urgent not merely for its importance on the battlefield, but because the reliance upon traditional methods for detonating artillery shells was wreaking havoc in the cities of Britain. Even when the time fuzes in artillery shells used by the British came from Switzerland, the land of the precision clock, there was a certain degree of unreliability. When the British were forced to rely on their own fuzes, the situation became disastrous. Jack Allen, who was working on the proximity fuze at the Cavendish Laboratories, said at the time that half the fuzes currently used in British artillery were defective and caused shells to explode only when they landed. He claimed that these shells might be killing as many Londoners as German bombs. If this was true, what would it mean in practice?

A total of 60,595 civilians were killed in the United Kingdom over the course of the Second World war by enemy action. Of this total, we can at once remove 8,042. These are the people killed by V 1s and V 2s. As we know, the AA guns which shot down these weapons were usually operating outside cities and so there are likely to be few, if any, instances of friendly fire among them. This leaves us with a total of 52,553 who were killed during air raids or other enemy action. If as many civilians really were being killed by anti-aircraft shells as were being killed by German bombs, that would mean that British artillery accounted for over 26,000 civilian deaths in Britain between 1939 and 1944. Of course, this might be a gross exaggeration, although we must bear in mind that

J.B.S. Haldane, writing in 1938, said pretty much the same thing about air raids in the First World War, namely that, 'In some raids they caused as many casualties as the enemy bombs'. We remember too, the headline in the *Derby Evening Telegraph* for 21 April 1943, which read 'MORE INJURED BY SHELLS THAN BOMBS'. It is by no means implausible that shells killed as many people as bombs.

We have established an upper limit for the death toll inflicted by the British artillery and a horrifying one it is too: 26,000 or more civilian deaths. What might the bare minimum figure be for the number of casualties caused in this way? This is almost impossible to guess at. When only a few bombs were dropped and the anti-aircraft fire was restrained, it was sometimes possible to find out exactly how each fatal casualty had died. In such cases, AA fire was usually implicated in at least 10 per cent of deaths and often more. In the course of one raid which killed less than 100 people, that of 17 January 1943, we know that of the 74 deaths, 23 were definitely caused by artillery shells. That's about a third of the total. We might take 10 per cent though as a convenient, rough-and-ready figure for the bare minimum proportion of deaths by friendly fire between 1939 and 1944. Even this would give us a total of about 5,500 civilians killed by the artillery operating on the British mainland.

In the Introduction, it was said that the story of the Blitz as we know it, the highly coloured and romanticized version which children are taught at school, conceals a terrible crime. This crime was the deliberate slaughter of thousands of unarmed men, women and children. Perhaps some readers felt that this was hyperbole, but a few moments consideration will soon show that it was nothing of the sort.

There was no conceivable military justification for the firing of heavy artillery into the skies above Britain's cities. The then Prime Minister, Winston Churchill, had inveighed against the practice during a previous world war and knew that it was at best useless and at worst likely to inflict heavy casualties on the civilian population. Nevertheless, he went ahead and ordered millions of shells to be launched over London and other cities, regardless of the inevitable deaths which would be caused.

The motive for the artillery barrages over Britain during the Second World War had nothing at all to do with shooting down aeroplanes: the sole aim was to prevent the wholesale flight of the civilian population from cities, thus crippling industrial production and hindering the ability to wage war. Nobody ever made any bones about this, at least until after the war had ended. The sound of the guns was reassuring and encouraged people to stay put in cities. It was a morale-boosting device and, as such, was enormously successful.

The plain fact is that the British city-dwellers intending to flee from their homes into the safety of the countryside were shelled by their army, on the direct orders of the government, so as to persuade them to change their minds and abandon their plans. That the artillery was not actually being aimed at them makes no difference at all, either legally or morally. If I discharge a deadly weapon in a reckless or haphazard fashion and somebody's death results from this, then I am culpable, whatever my actual intention. If I fire a gun over the heads of a group of people to scare them and the bullet kills somebody a mile away, I have committed murder. I might, with an exceptionally shrewd lawyer, argue the case down to manslaughter, but that I have committed a crime will never be in dispute. Legally and morally, the crime will be brought home to me if once I am caught.

In precisely the same way, the fact that the government ordered the army to fire shells which were intended to explode in the air, does not removed from them the responsibility for the many deaths which resulted from those orders. Somewhere between 5,000 and 50,000 British civilians were killed by their own guns during the Second World War and the responsibility for this series of massacres rests ultimately with Winston Churchill, the man who gave the orders and intervened on more than one occasion to ensure that they were being carried out. Nor is this the only aspect of the business where guilt for so many deaths may lay.

We know that, contrary to the commonly-perceived narrative, it was Britain which first began bombing German cities rather than the other way round. On 15 May 1940, weeks before the evacuation of Dunkirk and months before the Battle of Britain, the RAF launched a 135-plane bombing raid on Germany, striking the centre of Hamburg, among other places, with the resultant death of 34 civilians. This was four months before the beginning of the Blitz. The suggestion has been made that these early bombing attacks on German cities were a deliberate attempt to provoke Germany into retaliating and striking at the cities of Britain. By this reading of the situation, Churchill, who of course became Prime Minister just five days before the start of the raids on Germany, wished to ensure that air raids against Britain were limited to cities, to give the RAF time to build up their strength a little. After all, British strategy had for years been predicated upon a war where bombers pounded cities and this would have suited the British perfectly at such a critical stage of the war. The death of civilians would certainly hamper the war effort a good deal less than the destruction of airfields, fighters and radar installations.

It is difficult to believe that any British leader could have been so cold-blooded as to set out to lure enemy aircraft into killing the citizens of London in this way, but it would certainly make sense from a military viewpoint. If so, it would mean that Churchill was ultimately to blame for both the deaths from artillery and also those from the bombs themselves which were being dropped by the enemy, a startling thought indeed.

Although this book has not used a standard from of referencing, such as the Harvard system, the information contained in it has all been gleaned from reputable and authoritative sources. The Bibliography below lists the principle works consulted, but much information has also been taken from contemporary newspapers. The British Newspaper Archive is an online resource where, for a modest fee, hundreds of different newspapers may be examined and specific topics searched for. Anybody who wished to get a flavour of what was and was not known about anti-aircraft fire during the Second World War could do worse than to read what was being reported in various provincial newspapers.

For those interested to see in real life some of the artillery discussed in this book and also to visit one or two sites which have been mentioned, an appendix below lists some interesting places, all of which are open to the public.

Appendix: Places of Interest Relating to Anti-Aircraft Guns and their Use in Britain

There are a number of places where the different types of anti-aircraft guns mentioned in this book may be seen and sites associated with their use during the First and Second World War may be visited.

Mudchute Park & Farm
Pier Street
Isle of Dogs
London E14 3HP

Two particularly fierce barrages of anti-aircraft fire were set up over London during the Second World War, in locations which, it was feared, were being used as navigational markers by the Luftwaffe. One of these was Hyde Park and the other the Isle of Dogs. The concrete structures of one of those sites on the Isle of Dogs is not only intact, but a restored 3.7in gun of the kind used there in the war has been installed exactly where it would have been during the air raids on London. This is where to go if you wish to see just what an AA site would have looked like during the Blitz. The gun there may be seen in Illustration 4 of this book.

Tilbury Fort
No 2 Office Block
The Fort
Tilbury
Essex
RM18 7NR

This is another place where anti-aircraft guns may be seen at a place where they were actually in use. In 1903, some 3in naval guns were installed at Tilbury Fort. These guarded the Thames, in case enemy ships tried to attack London. These were the type of guns which were principally used in Britain during the First World War as anti-aircraft artillery. Two of these guns are still in place at Tilbury. A 3.7in gun from the Second World War is also to be found here. Anti-aircraft guns were fired from Tilbury Fort in both the First and Second World Wars, as it was along the route used by bombers and Zeppelins heading towards London.

HMS *Belfast*
The Queen's Walk
London
SE1 2JH
HMS *Belfast* is a cruiser from the Second World War, which is moored permanently on the Thames, in Central London. It has two kinds of anti-aircraft guns. One is the 40mm Bofors gun and the other dual-purpose 4in guns, which were the main naval anti-aircraft guns of the Second World War. Both types of guns were used in London at various times.

The Headquarters of the London Inner Artillery Zone Anti-aircraft Defences
206 Brompton Road
Knightsbridge
London
SW3 2BQ
From 1906 to 1934, there was a Tube station at Brompton Road, just around the corner from the museums of South Kensington. During the Second World War, this was the headquarters of anti-aircraft defences in London. Although the station closed down many years ago, it is quite possible to identify it by the maroon tiles which face the outside of the building. It was here that General Pile planned the use of the artillery which was positioned in and around London. The best view of the old station may be obtained from Cottage Place, which is next to the Brompton Oratory.

Imperial War Museum Duxford
Duxford
Cambridgeshire
CB22 4QF

This museum, sited at a former RAF base, has several anti-aircraft guns on display. In addition to a 3.7in gun and Bofors from the Second World War, it also has a 1lb 'pom-pom' gun, the first anti-aircraft gun ever deployed in Britain. This weapon was used extensively during the First World War.

The Battle of Britain Bunker
11 Group Operations Room
Wren Avenue
Uxbridge
UB10 0FD
The only RAF Fighter Group Operations Room open to the public. This museum is on the London Underground and, in addition to giving a vivid idea of what an RAF base would have been like during the Second World War, also contains a Bofors gun of the type used to defend airfields during the Battle of Britain and Blitz. This museum is of interest, for it was here that Winston Churchill was told by Air Vice-Marshal Park during the Battle of Britain that there were no reserves and that all available planes were in the air.

Royal Air Force Museum London
Grahame Park Way
London
NW9 5LL
An excellent place to visit for seeing aircraft which took part in the Battle of Britain. This museum also contains a 3.7in anti-aircraft gun in perfect condition.

RSPB Rainham Marshes
New Tank Hill Road
Purfleet
Essex
RM19 1SZ
The inclusion of a nature reserve run by the Royal Society for the Protection of Birds might surprise some readers, but there is a remarkable site to be visited here. A concrete blockhouse was erected here during the First World War to watch for submarines attempting to make their

way up the Thames. A .303in Vickers machine gun was mounted on the top and in March 1916, a Zeppelin was shot down by this.

Nothe Fort
Barrack Road
Weymouth
Dorset
DT4 8UF
During the Second World War, this coastal fort was home to four 3.7in anti-aircraft guns. One is still in position, along with various other artillery pieces.

Explosion! Museum of Naval Firepower
Heritage Way
Priddy's Hard
Gosport
Hampshire
PO12 4LE
Some of the defence of London and other cities was undertaken during the Second World War by using naval guns. This museum has an example of a gun turret, taken from a warship, which features twin 4.5in QF guns, of the type sometimes used for anti-aircraft fire. Other AA guns may be seen here, including a 3.7in gun.

Dover Castle
Castle Hill
Dover
Kent
CT16 1HU
Dover Castle boasts a unique example of a First World War 3in anti-aircraft gun which is in working order. It has been used to fire blanks and is on permanent display at the castle. There is also a 3.7in Second World War AA gun, although this is not in as good condition as some.

Chadwell Heath Anti-Aircraft Gun Site Conservation Area
Whalebone Lane
London Borough of Barking and Dagenham

It is perhaps a stretch of the imagination to describe this site as being open to the public, although it can be reached by those with an interest in the subject. Set on high ground, in the middle of fields and a quarry, is something of a time capsule. It is an entire anti-aircraft gun site from the Second World War, as intact as though it had been abandoned only yesterday. All the concrete structures and paths are intact and in good shape. The only damage is some modern graffiti. This site guarded the approach to London along the Thames. Those with a real interest in the subject will have no difficulty in locating and visiting this site, although the legal situation relating to trespass might deter some.

Bibliography

Begg, Paul (ed.), *City Walks of London*, Robson Books, 1990.

Brewer, Paul, *Chronicles of War*, Carlton Books, 2007.

Brown, Mike, *Put That Light Out! Britain's Civil Defences at War 1939–1945*, Sutton Publishing, 1999.

Carey, John (ed.), *The Faber Book of Reportage*, Faber & Faber, 1987.

Castle, Ivor, & Innes T. A. (eds), *Covenants with Death*, Daily Express Publications, 1934.

Collier, Basil, *The Defence of the United Kingdom*, Her Majesty's Stationery Office, 1957.

Cooksley, Peter, *The Home Front: Civilian Life in World War One*, Tempus Publishing, 2006.

Craven, Wesley Frank, & Cate, James Lea, *The Army Air Forces in World War II: Defense of the Western Hemisphere*, Washington DC Office of Air Force History, 1983.

Crawford, Steve, *Strange But True Military Facts*, Pen & Sword Books, 2010.

Davies, Norman, *Europe at War 1939–1945*, Macmillan, 2006.

Dickinson, W.N., *History of Anti-aircraft Guns*, Sagwan Press, 2018.

Doyle, Peter, *World War II in Numbers*, Bloomsbury Publishing, 2013.

Fountain, Michael (ed.), *World War II: The People's Story*, Readers Digest Association, 2003.

Frankland, Mark, *Radio Man: The remarkable rise and fall of C.O. Stanley (History and Management of Technology)*, Institution of Engineering and Technology, 2002.

Frankland, Noble, *The Encyclopaedia of 20th Century Warfare*, Mitchell Beazley, 1989.

Fredette, Raymond, *The Sky on Fire: The First Battle of Britain, 1917–1918*, Smithsonian Institution Press, 1966.

Gardiner, Juliet, *The Blitz: The British Under Attack*, HarperPress, 2010.

Gardiner, Juliet, *Wartime: Britain 1939–1945*, Headline Book Publishing, 2004.

Garnett, Mark, & Weight, Richard, *Modern British History*, Johnathon Cape, 2003.
Gilbert, Martin, *Descent in Barbarism: A History of the Twentieth Century 1933–1951*, HarperCollins, 1998.
Haldane, J.B.S., *Air Raid Precautions*, Victor Gollancz, 1938.
Hodgson, Vere, *Few Eggs and No Oranges*, Dennis Dobson, 1976.
Hogg, Ian V., *British and American Artillery of World War II*, Greenhill Books, 2002.
Horton, Edward, *The Age of the Airship*, Sidgwick & Jackson, 1973.
Levine, Joshua, *The Secret History of the Blitz*, Simon & Schuster, 2015.
London Police Pensioner Magazine, *London Police, Their Stories: 80 Years at the Sharp End*, Merlin Unwin Books, 1998.
Longden, Sean, *Blitz Kids*, Constable & Robinson, 2012.
Mack, Joanna, & Humphries, Steve, *The Making of Modern London 1939–1945: London at War*, Guild Publishing, 1985.
Marwick, Arthur, *The Home Front: The British and the Second World War*, Thames & Hudson, 1976.
Mawson, Gillian, *Voices from the Past: Britain's Wartime Evacuees*, Frontline Books, 2016.
Moberg, Stig H., *Gunfire!: British Artillery in World War II*, Frontline Books, 2017.
Mortimer, Gavin, *The Longest Night: 10–11 May 1941*, Weidenfeld & Nicolson, 2005.
Nixon, Barbara, *Raiders Overhead*, Lindsay Drummon, 1943.
O'Brien, Terence H., *Civil Defence*, Her Majesty's Stationery Office, 1955.
Parry, Simon W., *Beaufighter: The Photographic Story*, Red Kite, 2001.
Ray, John, *The Night Blitz*, Arms & Armour, 1996.
Rayner, Ed, & Stapley, Ron, *Debunking History*, Sutton Publishing, 2002.
Regan, Geoffrey, *Air Force Blunders*, Guinness Publishing, 1991.
Regan, Geoffrey, *More Military Blunders*, Guinness Publishing, 1993.
Salisbury, Harriet, *The War on Our Doorstep: London's East End and How the Blitz Changed it Forever*, Ebury Press, 2012.
Shuckburgh, Julian, *London Revealed: Uncovering London's Hidden History*, HarperCollins Publishers, 2003.
Spender, Stephen, *Citizens in War – And After*, George G. Harrap, 1945.
Storey, Neil R., *WRNS: The Women's Royal Naval Service*, Shire Publications, 2017.

Taylor, A.J.P., *The First World War*, Hamish Hamilton, 1963.
Taylor, John W.R., Taylor, Michael J. H., & Mondey, David (eds), *The Guinness Book of Air Facts & Feats*, Guinness Superlatives, 1970.
Taylor, Rosemary, & Lloyd, Christopher, *The East End at War*, Sutton Publishing, 2000.
Webb, Edwin, & Duncan, John, *Blitz Over Britain*, Spellmount, 1990.
Webb, Simon, *Myths That Shaped Us*, Pen & Sword Books, 2017.
Webley, Nicholas (ed.), *A Taste of Wartime Britain*, Thorogood Publishing, 2003.
Wells, H.G., *The War in the Air*, George Bell & Sons, 1908.
Withington, John, *Capital Disasters*, Sutton Publishing, 2003.

Index